Some Glad Morning

Some Glad Morning

HOLDING HOPE IN APOCALYPTIC TIMES

Rob McCall

PUSHCART

ISBN: 978-09600977-2-2

Pushcart Press
P.O. Box 380
Wainscott, New York 11975

Distributed by W.W. Norton Co.
500 Fifth Avenue
New York, New York 10110

Designed by Mary Kornblum

PRINTED IN THE UNITED STATES OF AMERICA

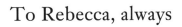

To Rebecca, always

CONTENTS

Summer

Autumn

Winter

Spring

Introduction

NOT SO LONG AGO, before the 2020 pandemic and before every year was hotter than the last, dire forecasts of doom were the domain of splinter groups of Revelation-besotted Christians, back-country tub-thumpers, and leather-lunged street-corner prophets. Today, visions of the end of the world are presented afresh daily to anyone who reads the morning news or follows on-line media. Even the venerable New York Times has been salting its sophisticated offerings with doses of apocalypticism. Eschatology, the study of the end-times and once a tiny dark corner of the obscure realm of theology, has been mainstreamed to the masses and the question of whether the world will end in fire or ice is parsed over coffee and at the dinner table, often with heated debates over the details. Suddenly those street-corner prophets aren't looking so crazy anymore.

Tragically, though, the deep chords of hope for a coming new age, which resound throughout ancient accounts of the end-times, are too often unheard on today's stage. Little attention is given to Nature's powers of healing. Little thought is given to how to weather the storms of market crashes or pandemics or global climate disruptions and sail on to the new world, or to what that new world could be like. As a result, many people are overcome and paralyzed by fear, rage and hopelessness. Depression, suicide, anxiety and addiction, including wealth addiction, are rampant and threaten to crumble industrialized societies from within, playing into the hands of demagogues and the greedy.

Some Glad Morning is aimed straight at this malaise. Arranged on the circle of the seasons, this small volume offers daily rations of wisdom from Nature, reflections on ancient texts and contemporary culture, and practical action, all gathered with the hope of feeding the soul and strengthening the heart for these times.

We are currently hearing far more prophecies of a dark and disastrous future for the planet than we are visions for global healing. This is to be expected, in large part because bad news sells. But it is also tragic because if our goal is to bring about change in ourselves or others, dread is a mighty poor motivator. It mostly causes us to withdraw and give up. Practical hope is a far better way to get us moving, creating a vision of the world as it could be, based on the past and present hopes and achievements of our species, and setting out to help make that vision happen.

I was raised on the Bible but my reliance on scripture in what follows is not an endorsement of dogmatic Christianity, any more than my reliance on the Tao Te Ching is an endorsement of Taoism as it is currently practiced, or my reliance on writers like Annie Dillard, Thomas Paine and Henry David Thoreau makes them saints to me. The world is gradually moving from dogmatic religion established by male hierarchies and based on supernatural revelation to open-sourced religion established by consensus and based on Nature. We are moving with it.

I took up the family trade of preaching in 1984 and finally arrived in Blue Hill, Maine in the Fall of 1986, preaching at the Congregational church there nearly every Sunday until my retirement in the Fall of 2014. In 1992 I started writing the Awanadjo Almanack as a column in the local paper and a short feature on community radio and it continues. The Almanack was founded on the idea that care and compassion for the Earth can be fostered, not so much by oceans of rhetoric or mountains of technical data, nor by frightening, shaming or blaming others for the sad state of things, but by encouraging love and delight in the Creation.

Anyone might wonder how it is that a bewildered Midwestern Yankee managed to find something to say about Spirit and Nature weekly for 30 or more years. It is simply a matter of keeping the eyes and heart open, because Nature herself has infinite wonders to reveal, and an abundance of spirit to loosen the tongue, guide the lost, and revive the weary. If I ever got stuck on how to say it, a hike up the trails on Awanadjo invariably got me unstuck.

Over the years, people have sometimes suggested that the Almanack has a cult following. If it does, it is the oldest cult in the world, because it follows the Old Faith that was practiced by the first people, and still is practiced today. It is the conviction that Nature is sacred and ought to be approached with love, wonder, and respect. The truth is not in this book you are holding, nor is it in the books I have quoted herein, nor in any other book. The truth is, as Paine said, "in the Creation we behold... It cannot be forged; it cannot be counterfeited; it cannot be lost; it cannot be altered; it cannot be suppressed. It does not depend upon the will of man whether it will be published or not. It publishes itself from one end of the earth to the other."

The truth is alive out there, and on the move.

As for the traditions, one of the most powerful visions of the future was seen by the prophet Isaiah who lived during the 8th century BCE, or thereabouts. He and his followers wrote the book of prophecy which bears his name. Forged out of apocalyptic war and captivity, exile and return, that book gives us timeless images of a Peaceable Kingdom where the wolf will dwell with the lamb and the calf with the lion, and a little child shall lead them. This imagery has matchless staying-power. Chances are good that we all heard random notes of this ancient and enduring vision floating in the air as recently as last Christmas or Easter.

For background, we look at two similar men with very different visions of the future drawn from the Bible.

Edward Hicks [1780-1849] was born in his grandparents' mansion in Bucks County Pennsylvania. His parents were Loyalists and Anglicans and lost everything in the Revolution. Young Edward had an artistic bent, and floundered some, describing himself as "a weak, wayward young man, exceedingly fond of singing, dancing, and vain amusements" not unlike other artists through the ages. He joined up with the Quakers when he was 23 and when he was 32 he became a traveling Quaker minister. To supplement his income, meager like most ministers in those times, he painted coaches and farm equipment, household furniture and tavern signs, and easel paintings to be hung on the wall.

Being Quaker, he became a bearer of the hopeful vision of the Peaceable Kingdom and the images of lions, lambs, and little children appeared again and again in his work. Often the child would be embracing the lion or the leopard, hanging his arm over its neck, or sitting on its back. Hicks painted the lion and the lamb and the child watching William Penn sign his treaty with the Indians. He painted them watching a caravan of Quakers passing by bedecked with banners calling for Peace on Earth. He painted them looking at a natural bridge over a river. He painted scores of Peaceable Kingdoms in many settings and sizes for the rest of his life. Over 60 versions from his hand have been found, and there may be still more out there tucked away in Pennsylvania attics or haylofts. This peaceful vision of time to come dominated Edward Hicks's imagination, his work, and his life.

Now look at William Miller [1782-1849] who was born in Western Massachusetts two years after Hicks was born and died in the same year—two men born in the same country and the same era, breathing the same air, and raised on the same Bible, both Christian preachers, both husbands and fathers, and both farmers, but with very different visions of the time to come. William Miller's father was a soldier, and Miller himself served as a constable, a deputy sheriff, a lieutenant in the militia, and then a combat soldier in the War of 1812, enduring brutal battlefield experiences. After the war, Miller became obsessed with the end of the world. Maybe it was post-traumatic stress, cast in a hard-shell Baptist mold.

Miller preferred the prophet Daniel whose vision was so horrible that it terrified even the prophet himself. Drawing on this terrifying vision, William Miller predicted that the earth and all sinners would be consumed by raging fire while the faithful would rise to meet Christ in the clouds sometime between March 21, 1843 and March 21, 1844. [Around this time, someone told Ralph Waldo Emerson that the world was coming to an end, whereupon he replied. "Very well, we'll get along without it."] When the year passed uneventfully, the earth didn't burn up and no sinners were immolated, Miller and his followers called it "The Great Disappointment," one of the more chilling of many historical examples of "Christian" ruthlessness.

Several generations of Miller's spiritual descendants have continued to predict the end of the world at a particular day and time, and their disappointment continues. However, if William Miller's vision of the end did not come to pass, it must be admitted that Edward Hicks's hasn't yet entirely, either. Yet Hicks's vision is widespread and foresees a more gradual change, a dream that creeps in more slowly from above and from below and from all sides, like the arrival of Spring. This is happening today world-wide.

This is the same dream of an earth renewed that was born in the imagination of Isaiah when his people were in exile. This is the same dream that Jesus dreamed; and Julian of Norwich, the dream that was danced around the cedar tree at Pine Ridge and Standing Rock, the same dream that Dr Martin Luther King Jr dreamed. It is the dream of the immigrant, the refugee, the homesteader, the small farmer, the environmentalist, and millions of others through time and around the world. It is the grass pushing up through the pavement, it is the sprout rising from the stump, it is the Earth healing itself, it is the Peaceable Kingdom. It is the dream of the Creator for the whole Creation.

This conviction is now reviving and building strength all over the world and will one day bring humanity to a new and better place, not as masters, but as caretakers of the Creation. That will be some glad morning.

SUMMER

Yearning and Turning

EVERY NOW AND THEN while I water the geraniums on the front porch, I give their pots a half turn so they won't get too lopsided from reaching out for the sun. Botanists call their way of growing toward the sun "heliotropism;" I call it 'yearning for the light'. Likewise, whether you plant it upside down, or downside up, a sprouting seed always sends its roots downward. Botanists call this "geotropism," but I call it 'yearning for the earth'. Sunflowers and daisies turn their pretty faces to follow the sun through the day. Potatoes imprisoned in the dark cellar send out pale, spindly shoots reaching toward the nearest window. Spruce roots split the rock. Grass pushes up through the pavement. Though it seems meek enough, this is a rock-splitting, earth-changing power. These yearnings are innate and unconscious and irrepressible. Everywhere in their great dance of rising branches, plants reach up to the light. Everywhere in their stolid stance, they reach down through the ground as though their very lives depended upon it. They cannot see, but they are not blind.

I believe we are born with similar yearnings and reachings, and though some may try, these yearnings cannot be denied or erased. Just as the flower naturally turns toward the sun, we naturally turn toward the justice, righteousness and peace of God's kingdom. Though others may try to satisfy our yearnings with falsehoods, the hunger returns and can only be satisfied by the truth. No flat screen or image of an image of an image can satisfy our longing for the one true light.

Likewise, just as the tree sends its roots down, we reach for the ground of our being. We ache to touch the source of life, smell it, walk on it, lie down on it. No sidewalk or high-rise or parking lot or museum can satisfy this yearning. The ongoing uprisings and revolutions around the world are the acting out of those same hungers. The yearning for justice and righteousness, and for some ground of one's own, will not be bought off, or put to sleep, or paved over for long. It will reach for the light again and again and forever, pushing aside all that would keep it down.

This spirit of putting down roots and reaching for the light has always found a home in New England, whose rocky soil gave birth to political revolution, industrial revolution, abolitionism and the labor union movement. By the turn of the 20th century New England had been hunted out, logged out and farmed out; her rivers were poisoned, and her youth had fled at Horace Greeley's call to "go west, young man."

But in the early 21st century this region is looking more and more like a model for the gradual resurrection of a once exploited and depleted ecosystem. I don't want to sound overly optimistic but we will note that New England is seeing a resurgence in formerly endangered animals. Her rivers are clean again. Her forests are renewed. She is a fountainhead of innovation and creativity. And best of all, the young are returning to her small towns and farms to give them a new lease on life and a new hope not seen in our lifetimes.

As it is today, so it has been since the beginning: the irrepressible hungering and thirsting for justice and righteousness and a piece of God's kingdom, the unstoppable reaching for the light and the unquenchable yearning for the earth—men and women, children and youth like trees walking.

Walking Trees

THIS BRINGS US to the enchanting story in the gospel of Mark about a man whose sight was restored by Jesus. How profound was the vision of 'men like trees walking' he saw for a brief moment after his vision returned and before the veil of the ordinary fell again over his eyes, so that he saw men simply as men and trees as trees, like everyone else. What a penetrating first glimpse of the mystery of life on earth he got.

This miracle of a man receiving his sight is mirrored by the miracle of every tree. Left alone, the green cell combines sunlight, water and nourishment from the soil to make more and more life. Animals, in turn, derive their life from plants. A big tree is the actual breathing incarnation of this miracle. This goes a long way towards explaining why the Tree of Life is mentioned at the beginning and end of the Bible and several times in between, and why trees are honored around the world and in every major religion. Shinto priests bring offerings to big trees in the mountains of Japan and tree-huggers live in the tops of giant redwoods in California to protect them from felling.

In my saunters around town I have found a number of exceedingly large specimens: a yellow "Getchell" birch halfway up the mountain surrounded by a grove of its offspring, a sugar maple on Pleasant Street in the village, and a huge white ash near Closson's in North Blue Hill, to name a few. It is hard to pass by one of these giants without admiring it, speaking to it and even hugging it and feeling the pulse of its surging sap pressing against your heart. These heroes have successfully weathered the storms of far more than a human lifetime and they humble us with their great mass and age, their constancy, their productivity and their peaceful patience. They deserve to be honored as icons and monuments to the majesty of life on earth.

Around here the trees are now fully leafed out and the world is green, green, green as far as the eye can see where not long ago all was gray and brown and barren. It is astounding to think that these billions of leaves, this huge bio-mass of vernal flesh, has all appeared in the last few weeks where before there were bare branches, all manufactured simply out of water, sunlight and CO_2 by multitudes of vegetative creatures from the smallest grasses to the largest trees. It is astounding!

How is it that every leaf looks like every other of its kind and different from other kinds? Where are the plans, where are the secret blueprints, where are the instructions by which these infinite and intricate food factories are designed and built to feed the whole Creation? It is this simple process that is the engine of nearly all life on our vast green and blue planet. Every leaf, seed, stalk, nut, grain, berry, fruit or nectar eaten by every creature in the world is created by this same simple process now unfolding right before our eyes. I am dumbfounded, flabbergasted, stymied and stupefied at the miracle of it all. How can anyone even eat a stalk of celery anymore—never mind mow the grass—while millions of its cousins are watching?

Fortunately, the pace of lawn mowing has slowed a little as the season progresses, but many of us are still out there at least once a week making a huge racket, blowing fumes, increasing our carbon footprint and pulverizing innocent green living things. America has a lawn fetish and you'd better have one too or risk being shunned as unpatriotic; and your author, despite all his high talk, is out there mowing with the rest of them. My theory is that the lush, close-cropped greensward we crave harkens back to Neolithic times when we were herders and when wide open spaces grazed close to the ground spelled security and happiness for our ancestors in the form of meat. All of this mowing is done by the ancient ghost of Man the Herder and Man the Farmer mindlessly trying to return to those days of yore when we really did grow our own food, now produced largely by distant agribusinesses subsidized by billions of our tax dollars.

Meanwhile, the production of bio-fuels, making corn and other edible plants into ethanol to be consumed as fuel, while world food prices climb and the poor starve, is a moral outrage of the highest magnitude. Who could imagine a greater atrocity than the well-to-do burning the food supply of the poor so that we can fly to Disneyland or Dubai, or drive the kids to soccer practice and the cat to the vet? But that is exactly what is happening. Dependence on fossil fuels to run the global economy is approaching a dead end. Estimates of fuel calories required to produce food calories today run as high as 10 fuel calories to raise one food calorie. Peasants all over the world are fleeing the land which has fed them sustainably for thousands of years to work in urban factories making sneakers and shirts for pennies a day.

It's hard to imagine a soft landing for this ill-fated flight, but your commentator, ever the optimist, believes that there is reason for hope in the long term. As we see the infrastructure of the global economy coming apart, we are also seeing the infrastructure of local economy coming together.

CHARLES DARWIN 1809-1882:
If the misery of the poor be caused, not by the laws of nature, but by our institutions, great is our sin.

Talking Plants

WE TEND TO THINK of plants as being motionless unless blown by the wind or moved by some other outer force, although, there are Venus fly traps, mail-ordered by generations of boys hoping to watch them gobble a fly. But, we think, moving plants, in Maine? No way. Then maybe we happen to walk by a clump of daisies a few times and notice how their faces follow the sun across the sky. Or we watch the tall sunflowers in our garden do the same, turning, turning through the day, adoring their deity. Even slower is the movement of climbing plants in our gardens; pole beans, sweet peas, grape vines, morning glories. When we walk through the garden in the dewy morning we notice that they are not holding the same position they were the night before. Time-lapse video shows them reaching longingly up and out in all directions, and then wrapping themselves around a twig or pole or arbor as they climb higher. These plant motions are slow and graceful, but they are most certainly movement. Some plants here in Maine move much faster than this.

I will never forget one hot dry summer day coming down the mountain and hearing what sounded like raindrops falling all around. I could even feel them hitting my clothes. Looking up at a clear blue sky, then down to the ground around about, I soon discovered what was happening. I was walking through a patch of lupines which were furiously expelling their seeds. As I stood still I could hear the pattering while the lupine pods suddenly burst and flung their tiny seeds recklessly far and wide. Common bladderwort *Utricularia vulgaris* and horned bladderwort *Utricularia cornatus* are aquatic plants, fairly common in Maine, with single yellow blossoms looking a bit like a snapdragon. As benign and gentle as it might appear, however, bladderwort is a meat-eater.

It has capsules on its underwater roots that open instantly when touched, sucking in small creatures unfortunate enough to have come too close: Daphnia, nematodes, tadpoles, mosquito larvae and even small fish fry. For his whole life, Charles Darwin was fascinated by the motion of plants. His next to last volume was called *The Power of Movement in Plants* published in 1880. Plants that move! What next? Plants that talk? Plants that feel?

Well, yes, apparently. A 2019 study at Tel Aviv University found that plants emit ultrasonic noises when they are under stress. When they were not watered or when their stems or leaves were cut or torn, tobacco and tomato plants made sounds that, though too high-pitched for the human ear, could be picked up by microphones, and presumably heard by other plants and animals like mice and bats and possibly insects.

With this as background, gardens are starting to yield now with fresh spinach, lettuce, radishes and other greens; strawberries are delighting everyone young and old. Maybe you'll find some fresh u-pick peas if you are lucky. But will you want to pick them? The Farmer's Market bustles with growers and buyers alike. Support local farmers so they can continue to support you. Meanwhile apples are sizing up in the orchards and blueberries on the barrens; and so many other varieties of berries are plumping up in the fields and forests waiting for the intrepid forager to find them.

There is food enough for all if no one takes more than they need.

FROM GEORGE WASHINGTON CARVER 1861?-1943:
Anything will give up its secrets if you love it enough. Not only have I found that when I talk to the little flower or the little peanut, they will give up their secrets, but I have found that when I silently commune with people, they will give up their secrets too… Anything will talk to you if you love it enough.

Souling

WHEN I WAS GROWING UP in the '50s we listened to classical music and Broadway musicals at home and European hymns and anthems in church. I played violin in junior high and high school orchestras. That was my musical world and it didn't change until I got a transistor radio for 8th grade graduation. Little did my parents know what they were doing. I discovered the world of top 40 pop and rock & roll—very danceable [which I couldn't do] and singable [which I could]. But I still had no hint of the glorious universe of American music until I heard Harry Belafonte, Odetta, the Kingston Trio, and Pete Seeger in my mid-teens, and I knew from that moment what kind of music I loved. I have spent the rest of my life exploring this vast and soulful musical landscape. By the time I was 18 I was soaking up Country and Bluegrass by day and playing in honky-tonks, coffeehouses, street corners—and just about anywhere else—-by night. When I first heard Hank Williams sing "I'm So Lonesome I Could Cry" I could honestly say I had never heard anything more brokenhearted and sorrowful in my entire life. And when I heard Dolly Parton sing "Tennessee Mountain Home" I had never heard anything more joyful and hopeful.

It's unfortunate for all of us to ignore the suffering of others, to gloss it over or blame them or send them away the way the rich man sent away the beggar Lazarus. But that can never work, because that suffering is real and it is everywhere and it is here to stay; even in us, if we look honestly there. That's what makes this music so great. It can face the suffering head on without looking away, and still be joyful too.

Paul says, "We know that the whole Creation, every creature, groans in travail and pain. And not only they, but ourselves also, waiting for the redeeming of our bodies by hope." In this world, we forever look for a way to address the suffering of ourselves and other creatures.

One answer is Soul. We may be accustomed to think of soul as a material thing that we have, an organ like the heart, or a faculty like the mind that disappears when we die. Or, we may think that soul is something spiritual, with no substance, yet that never dies. But, perhaps Soul is not either material or spiritual, but both. Perhaps Soul is the solution to the old mind/body problem. Let's take a closer look.

Did the unimaginable cataclysm we call the Big Bang, the moment that the cosmos decided to be rather than not be, did it hurt? Did it cause suffering? I feel that it did. Do the orderly movements of planets and the solar system feel good? Do they create joy? I feel so. Does Spring feel good to the earth, and Winter hurt? I feel so.

Suffering and joy are not exclusively human feelings, they are the emotions, the feelings of the Creation. When energy gave birth to matter at the Big Bang, it must have hurt. Imagine the pains of labor multiplied a billion-fold. Yet, at the moment matter was born, the capacity for infinite joy was born too. When God said, "Let there be light," joy and suffering were born together. Incarnation came at that moment, spirit expressed itself in substance, in taking on real bodies.

The voice, the expression, of incarnation is Soul, the embracing and bearing of both the joy and the suffering coming from the desire of the cosmos to be, rather than not to be. Soul is the echo of the sound of energy being expressed in matter. It is the song of spirit taking on flesh, joy and suffering together.

Listen to country and soul and gospel music. Listen to Sam Cooke, Tina Turner, Aretha Franklin. "To turn Soul music into Gospel music," they say, "you just take out the word 'Baby' and put in the word 'Jesus.'" Listen to blue-eyed soul: Hank Williams, Loretta Lynn, Bill Monroe, Peter, Paul & Mary, Janis Joplin.

Listen to the Song of Mary, "My soul magnifies the Lord and my spirit rejoices…" Listen to the howl of the wolf and the loon, the wail of the porcupine, the chant of the thrush, the song of the whale. This is Soul.

When Soul embraces both the joy and the suffering of life, it re-enacts and reaffirms the birth of the Creation. So long as it chooses to live only in its joy or only in its suffering, the soul remains stunted and small; and turns away from the Creation, the Incarnation, the Big Bang, the Big Birth, the time to laugh and the time to weep, the time to dance and the time to mourn. When the soul ignores the irresistible urge of energy to become matter and spirit to become flesh, then it turns away from the suffering and joy, the passion of Jesus, and the world, as it was and is and will be.

Our Teacher said, "Whoever will save his life will lose it, and whoever will lose his life for my sake shall find it." What would you give in exchange for your soul?

Unless we will bear in our bodies and souls both the joy and the suffering of real life in the real world, we cannot live in the fullness of the whole Creation. We will remain incompletely born and unredeemed. Yet, if we will lose our lives in the greater life, we will find life.

"Call the world, if you please," wrote John Keats in a letter to his family, "call the world… the vale of soul-making."

Our bodies may be the source of our pain, but they can also be the source of our joy. If our bodies are dwelling in pain but not in joy, in fear but not in hope, they remain not fully born, and unfinished. We are children of the Big Birth, the Big Bang, the travail of Creation, the Incarnation. We are an echo of the Creation's desire to be, to take on flesh and live in the harsh realities of both joy and suffering, like the loon, the wolf, the porcupine, the hermit thrush, the humpbacked whale, and the Christ.

Our bodies are not one thing or the other, joy or suffering, fear or hope, right or left. They are the joining of both. Look at how they are formed. We have two legs, two arms, two eyes, left and right. We have two lungs, two kidneys on the left and right. But we have one brain, one stomach and one heart, all in the center. [Of course, as Wm. Sloane Coffin said, "The heart is a little to the left."]

Why does God allow suffering in the world? I would say that God does not *allow* suffering, God *redeems* suffering. Where was God when Christ suffered on the Cross? God was crucified. Where was God at Dachau and Buchenwald and Auschwitz? God was in the gas chambers. Where was God at Hiroshima and Nagasaki? God was blinded and burned. Where was God on 9/11? God was in the falling buildings. Where is God in Iraq and Afghanistan and Syria? God is in the body-bags. This is the promise. Not that suffering will end, but that God will be there to provide all the Soul we need to redeem any suffering.

When he was in his early 60s, W.B. Yeats, the great Irish poet, wrote:

An aged man is but a paltry thing,
A tattered coat upon a stick, unless
Soul clap its hands and sing, and louder sing
For every tatter in its mortal dress.

A Pentecostal hymn written in 1899 by Ada Blenkhorn was recorded in 1928 by the Carters, still the first family of American country music:

There's a dark and a troubled side of life
There's a bright and a sunny side too
Though we meet with the darkness and strife,
The sunny side we also may view.

Would we rather live only in our joy or only in our sorrow? Or abandon every other creature, and not live at all? Listen to the soulful creatures. Listen to the promise of all the prophets. Along with the joys and sorrows of incarnation, we are offered ample grace and power to live it out in the flesh. We are offered incarnation with all of its joy and sorrow. And, if we take it, we are offered resurrection. We are even, each one of us, offered the power to ease the suffering of others by the sound of the song of our souls.

High Summer

*These things from ancient times arise from One: The sky is whole
and clear. The earth is whole and firm. The spirit is whole
and strong. The valley is whole and full. The ten thousand things
are whole and alive. The rulers are whole, and the country is
upright. All these are in virtue of wholeness.*

TAO TEH CHING C. 550 BC

AS AUGUST APPROACHES so does that time we call "high summer."
The grass is high, the trees reach high, the clouds reach even
higher, and the traffic and the price of lobster are pretty high too.
Maybe that's why it's called "high summer."

As the first waves of iconic summer wildflowers bloom and
fade—including dandelions, daisies, buttercups, lupine—the second wave comes on strong—including black-eyed Susan, Queen
Anne's lace, evening primrose, tansy and fireweed. Their many
shapes and colors, their intricate patterns and 'fearful symmetry'
are all designed for the enticement of pollinators and the production of fertile seeds—a devotion both fierce and beautiful to the
continuance of life here on our blue-green planet.

The steady and harmonious rhythms and rounds of Nature—
day and night, summer and winter, cold and heat, seedtime and
harvest—have always offered comfort in the face of mankind's
madness, selfishness, greed, murder and mayhem. Through it all,
Nature has held fast, immutable and immovable, our refuge and
strength in time of trouble. Thus, the idea of climate change is so
disturbing to so many, causing some to stand up stoutly and shout
their denials, and others to fall down moaning with their boundless
burdens of guilt. In these times, it is good to recall that all of our
religious traditions hold to the truth that what we do does affect
Nature. When we act in harmony with her, she offers peace and
abundance. When we act against her, she responds with chaos and

brokenness. We reap what we sow.

That is why so many of us do our best to lessen our carbon foot-print, recycle, repurpose, and reuse, or as our grandparents used to say, "use it up, wear it out, make it do, or do without." But while we recycle our few cans and bottles and newspapers, avoid excess traveling, turn down the heat, we also call out the bigger villains: the really big smoke-makers, the coal-burners, the frackers, the spillers, the mega-waste-makers, the sea-dumpers, the strip min-ers, the mountaintop-removers, and the market-manipulators. We do not forget who is making the big money from the on-going assault on Nature. As disturbing as this is, though, it is also good to remember that it takes time to turn the tide. But it will turn, and we will help turn it.

FROM K'UNG FU TZU OR CONFUCIUS C. 520 BC:
If there is righteousness in the heart, there will be beauty in the character. If there is beauty in the character, there will be harmony in the home. If there is harmony in the home, there will be order in the nations. When there is order in the nations, there will be peace in the world.

FROM BELLA ABZUG 1920-1998:
As women we know that we must always find ways to change the process, because the present institutions want to hold onto power and keep the status quo.

All Animals and Plants Have Their Purpose

All living creatures and all plants are a benefit to something.
Certain animals fulfill their purpose by definite acts. The
crows, buzzards, and flies are somewhat similar in their use,
and even the snakes have a purpose in being.

OKUTE, TETON SIOUX, 1911

"HELIOTROPE," AS IT IS CALLED around here, is going by along the mid-coast but still in bloom way Down East with its six foot tall fluted stems tinted red at the nodes, pinnate leaves, and clusters of aromatic white flowers with a tinge of purple. We say goodbye to another of the sweet, sweet presentations of summer. Botanists agree that this plant is not a heliotrope at all, but rather Valerian [*valeriana officianalis*], from which the highly effective herbal concoction Valerian root is drawn. Its pharmaceutical approximation is Valium, a widely used muscle-relaxant and anti-depressant.

With no knowledge of either the herbal or the pharmaceutical applications of this stately plant, it seems to your commentator that the sinfully rich aroma alone confers an intoxicating sense of joy and well-being, to the point that I begin to feel guilty walking near a stand of the plant. I find myself stooping down surreptitiously and inhaling forcefully, then looking around to see if anyone has noticed. Soon I am losing my train of thought, staring at the bright sky, and feeling the day's plans slipping away while I am hypnotized by the voluptuous odor, the healing balm of summer.

Perhaps to punish us for this pleasure, Mother Nature is presenting us with hordes of earwigs *[forficula auricularia]*. These flat, red-brown, nocturnal creatures—some nearly an inch long, with an elongated abdomen appended with a pair of fierce, crescent-shaped pincers look a little like a large ant designed by Salvador Dali or Stephen King. When we move anything outdoors, the earwigs come pouring out in droves. I swore for many years that earwigs did not bite or sting. That conviction ended abruptly not long ago when one got under my clothing and gave me a couple of good pinches in hidden places.

So, yes, they infest our houses and yards, they move fast, they run like cockroaches. Yes, they pinch, they swarm in hoards, they leave dusty droppings and a foul odor. But, they have also their holy purpose for being here, and their essential job to do even if we haven't the faintest idea what it is. Further, they are only with us for a brief two months. And, most winsome of all, we have it on good report that—unlike other non-social insects, and even some humans for that matter—earwigs care for their young. That's right. The female guards the eggs and watches over them until they are hatched and are big and nasty enough to fend for themselves. You have to admire them for that.

Eider ducklings are scurrying about under the watchful eyes of their mothers. The male eiders now become absentee fathers by moving out to deeper water, while the mothers and young stay closer to shore feeding on mussels and diving to avoid the swooping attacks of hungry eagles and ospreys. Young harbor seals are growing fast and turning from their infant blond and spotted coloration to a darker brown. On the gravel shore at our camp on Cobscook Bay, I found the forlorn cranium of an unfortunate infant seal with the soft folds of its brain molded on the inside of the skull where once the wisdom of the great waters was cradled.

FROM JOHN MUIR:
Nature's object in making animals and plants might possibly be first of all the happiness of each one of them, not the creation of all for the happiness of one. Why should man value himself as more than a small part of the one great unit of creation? And what creature of all that the Lord has taken the pains to make is not essential to the completeness of that unit - the cosmos? The universe would be incomplete without man; but it would also be incomplete without the smallest transmicroscopic creature that dwells beyond our conceitful eyes and knowledge.

Creature Chorus

Thou dost cause the grass to grow for the cattle and plants for man to cultivate, that he may bring forth food from the earth and wine to gladden the heart of man, oil to make his face shine, and bread to strengthen man's heart.

FROM PSALM 104

AS I WAS HEADING up the trail on a mild morning, it seemed that the mountain suddenly began talking to me. A sudden rush of words came pouring into my head full of new ideas and new perspectives on things. It was like listening to someone far wiser than myself gently but firmly teaching me what I needed to know. This has happened to me before. Maybe it has happened to you, too. This time, the mountain was expounding on the theory of evolution whereby the organisms which survive and thrive are those that best adapt to their environment.

"But what is the environment?" said the mountain. "It is not a thing. It is every thing above and below, near and far, active and inactive, living and non-living, seen and unseen. It is made up of all weather, every stone, every grain of sand, every cloud or drop of water, every living thing. Any change in one calls for change in all.

"The scene is not of a bloody battle for survival with only a few winners, so much as it is an age-old worldwide creature chorus swelling in song with every member constantly tuning its pitch and shading its volume to every other, to create the most pleasing and beneficent harmony, embracing and enhancing all, ever richer, ever more beautiful. Some voices sing high so others sing low, some are silenced while others are added; some rise while others fall, some sing the descant while some hum the bass, some die so that others can live. It is the music of the spheres, and the Director is also the Composer who hears from within and thrills with delight."

So the mountain seemed to say that day.

FROM CHARLES DARWIN 1809-1882:

There is grandeur in this view of life, with its several powers, having been originally breathed into a few forms or into one; and that, whilst this planet has gone cycling on according to the fixed law of gravity, from so simple a beginning endless forms most beautiful and most wonderful have been, and are being, evolved.

FROM WM. BUTLER YEATS:

Come, Fairies, take me out of this dull world, for I would ride with you upon the wind and dance upon the mountains like a flame!

Pilgrims

*Water flows from high in the mountains. Water runs deep in
the earth. Miraculously water comes to us and sustains all life.
Water flows over these hands. May I use them skillfully to
preserve our precious planet.*

FROM THICH NHAT HANH

THE DOG DAYS OF SUMMER begin on July 3 and go on until August
11, according to the Old Farmer's Almanac, never known for
stretching things a little bit or making things up. The Dog Days
are usually hot and muggy enough to make even the dogs uncom-
fortable, but they seem to be off to a slow start on that account,
at least here on Moose Island, where it has been cool at night and
warm during the day; perfect summer weather, and no mosquitoes
or blackflies either, at least according to the Awanadjo Almanack,
also not widely known for stretching things or making things up.

This quarter moon, along with bird-watching and whale-watch-
ing, we are watching the peak seasonal migration of the pink
tourist. About now the flocks arriving from the South are reaching
their greatest numbers and will likely continue until late August.
Some identifying characteristics include loud and repeated honking, wearing fairly funny T-shirts, and standing still in the middle
of the sidewalk and looking around. There was a time when anyone
asking for directions would be immediately identified as a tourist,
but today GPS has pretty much put an end to that, also depriving
locals of a little sport once enjoyed by giving tourists long, complicated—or even false—directions. Though a non-native species,
the tourist is essential to the local economy along the coast.

The produce of the fields is coming to your local farmer's
market with fragrant onions, heady lettuces, crunchy snow peas,
aromatic spices, and cut flowers to take home. Nearly every town
has a farmer's market with bright colorful booths, friendly earthy

people, and often live music, giving the whole enterprise the air of a medieval marketplace—or a Neolithic one, for that matter—feeding something very primal and deep in the heart. Support your farmer's market.

On a hot summer day there is nothing like a dip in saltwater to wash your cares away. Maine's waters are notoriously cold even in July, but that doesn't mean we can't jump right in, even if we are just going to jump right back out again. The astringent sting of salt in every little cut or scrape, the cold shock going in and the wave of warmth coming out, the smell and taste of the ocean water as it runs out of our hair, the refreshment and exhilaration: these are the rewards of a dip in the waters of the mighty Gulf of Maine.

We can tease and joke all we want about the tourists who come from a distance to visit for a few days, but it's good to remember that many of them are arriving here on a pilgrimage. They are looking for holy places. They are coming from cities and towns and places where the sacred is in such short supply that it is kept in large, steepled boxes with big brass locks, to be doled out in small samples and savored for an hour or so a week, places where the sacred is imprisoned in temples made by man surrounded on all sides by the secular. They come here to see sacred places that are wild, that are unbound, and they bring to these places a reverence that too many of us may be in danger of losing, seeing them day in and day out as we do. It's good to remember they are pilgrims.

FROM A HASIDIC SAYING:
When you walk across the field with your mind pure and holy, then from all the stones, and all growing things, and all animals, the sparks of their soul come out and cling to you, and then they are purified and become a holy fire within you.

AND FROM RACHEL CARSON:
If a child is to keep his inborn sense of wonder, he needs the companionship of at least one adult who can share it.

Being Still

THE PSALM SAYS TO "Be still, and know that I am God." "Be still!" we might say, "How can anyone be still anytime during the summer around here?: Busiest traffic of the whole year, no place to park, long lines at the bank and the PO, cookouts and cocktail parties and weddings, visitors from away: how could anyone find time to be still and know God?"

This is just the outward velocity and confusion of summer. Then there is the inward turmoil. How can we succeed without working harder? How can we accomplish more without being busier? How can we get ahead in our chosen field without moving faster? If we let down our guard for a minute, someone will take our place. I see it in the summer visitors who drive faster than the locals. They talk on their cell phones while lying in the hammock behind the Inn. They jog frantically up and down the road in their jogging suits. They work hard, and then they play hard. But it's all hard. The other day there were at least eight people—none of whom I recognized—sitting around outside the library waiting for it to open while working feverishly away on their lap-tops while ostensibly on vacation. "Wherever you go," said the sage, "there you are."

...Turmoil on the outside, turmoil on the inside, summer, winter, spring and fall. So it's not just about the seasons of the year. It's about the seasons of the soul, too. Now, maybe things are more intense these days than they've ever been and that's the price we pay for being on the "cutting edge of Western Civilization." Or maybe things haven't changed all that much in the last 2,000 years. Let's take a look at our teacher here.

"Hold it," says someone in the back. "I caught you right there trying to sneak up on us with our dose of Jesus, like hiding the dog's heartworm medication in a big piece of cheese so he'll gobble

it right down without noticing. Well, we're smarter than the dog."
To which your preacher responds, "Certainly you are smarter than
the dog, but it's still good for you to take your medicine." So, as I
said, let's take a look at Jesus here.

Is it unfair to compare Jesus and his times to us and our
times? Maybe. But, if anything, we come off having it far easier.
Remember, it wasn't just his career or reputation or earning power
or self-esteem that were on the line. It was his flesh and blood,
his body. It was his very life. This could be the ultimate stress. In
Matthew 11, Jesus has sent out his disciples to preach the overturning of the present order and the coming of a new kingdom.
You could call it 'regime change.' Instead of Satan being in charge
of this world, God is in charge. This is, of course, not good news
to the powers-that-be. Rather than change themselves, they prefer
to kill the messenger, which is why his cousin John the Baptist,
preaching the same new kingdom, has been thrown into Herod's
prison from which few, if any, come out alive. Next, Jesus is going
from town to town saying, "Woe to you if you don't change your
ways…" This is not vacationland. This is not R & R that Jesus is
doing. This is putting his life on the line.

Next, Jesus is engaging in defiant acts of civil disobedience. He
is deliberately and publicly challenging the religious law by pick-
ing and eating grain and healing the sick on the Sabbath to show
that in the new kingdom where we are now living, hungry and sick
people cannot be just written off by the powerful. Next, he is healing, then he is defending himself against the Pharisees, then he is
preaching again. It is highly stressful and exhausting just reading
about it. Now, abruptly in the text we find a strange interlude with
a strikingly different feel and tone, as different as stone and water.

That is why this peaceful interlude is so striking. In the twin-
kling of an eye here, Jesus goes from a hard ranting polemic on
God's judgment to a soft, mystical soliloquy on the secret knowledge and experience of 'the Father.' He goes from condemning

sinners to offering rest and relief from the yokes and burdens and labors of the world. This peaceful and poetic passage seems to have fallen right out of the sky, and maybe it has. But, here's what I think is happening:

We are told over and over again that when things get the most difficult and trying for Jesus, he withdraws to a quiet place. Not when it is most convenient; not when he has an opening in his schedule; not when everyone else is OK, but in the thickest tangle of turmoil when people are expecting the most of him, he takes a time out. Really. From the temptations in the wilderness at the beginning of his public career to the garden of Gethsemane at the end of it and many times in between, Jesus simply drops everything, walks away from it all and takes time to be still and know God. I think that is what happened here.

It's just what we'd better be doing too, now and in every season. We brush our teeth everyday and we go to the doctor regularly for the health of our bodies. We need to go to our Maker just as much for the health of our souls. It's the mystical union, it's the practice of the Presence. It's simply going there.

We can't expect the Spirit to drag us out of our Immensely Important Summer Schedules and say, "Hey! Hold it!" In fact, we'd probably prefer that She not do that, because when She does it can be awfully abrupt. But the Spirit is willing to come toward us gently if we are willing to come gently toward Her. "Draw nigh unto God," reads the scripture, "and He will draw nigh unto you." "Stretch out Your hand to help us," prays the 9th century mystic John Scotus Eriugena, "who cannot without You come to You." We take a step toward God, God takes a step toward us, and before we know it we are held in the most tender possible embrace.

After his prayer of thanks, Jesus rhapsodizes about the intimacy with 'the Father' which comes from this embrace. It is then that we see the striking change that has come over him. Just a moment before he was in a lofty and adamantine rage at the sins of the people around him. Now he is lowly and gentle of heart, offering—actually begging—to bear the burdens of others because Another has borne his. The transformation is absolutely stunning.

…Just as stunning as it can be for us if we will take time out from all our to-ing and fro-ing, our ranting and raging to be still and get with the Source of our being. When the tangled turmoil is most intense, that's when we most need to take a time out. When we don't have the time to, that's when it's time to. When we just can't, that's when we just must. There is a fountain of living water there that will quench the deepest thirst on a hot summer day far better than anything from Poland Spring. There is manna from heaven there that will satisfy a hungry heart fully as well as Maine's Acadia, or Katahdin, or Rangeley. We can go from a lofty and raging rant to a lowly and gentle heart with the speed of sound: the sound of the Spirit saying, "Be still, be still and know that I am."

ELIZABETH LAWRENCE 1904-1985:
Even if something is left undone, everyone must take time to sit still and watch the leaves turn

Grace

WE ARE MORE LIKELY to know about some horrible thing that happened a thousand miles away than a good thing that happened in our own neighborhood. Why is this? Why all the bad news flowing into our hearts everyday? Well, studies continue to show that people who are anxious actually buy more things than people who are not anxious. This goes a long way toward explaining why there is so much bad news being reported every day. Bad news sells.

Some have called ours the 'Age of Anxiety.' We are told that we are fighting an endless war against terror, and we numbly and passively agree. We are told that our savings are not enough to get us through retirement, or our children will leave college with massive debt and no job, or the planet is dying. Generalized anxiety disorders, panic attacks, post-traumatic stress syndrome, obsessive-compulsive disorder, histrionic personality disorder, fear, and worry are all on the list of modern maladies. Medications and talk therapy are the preferred treatments. The list of pharmaceuticals prescribed for anxiety is long and the names exceedingly strange. Depending on whose authority you accept, estimates of the numbers who suffer from pathological anxiety vary from a fairly small 3-4% of the population or 4-5 million, up to 40 million or 18% which would make it the most common mental illness in our country. Add in the physical ailments traceable to on-going stress caused by anxiety, worry and fear, and you have a major pathology spreading across the population.

Fears of global environmental collapse, natural disasters, deadly pandemics, terrorist attacks, personal sickness or injury, or losing a loved one are on the front pages and on the minds of many of us these days. Beneath all of these crouches the deep anxiety about our own suffering or death or the suffering and death of someone we love.

But perhaps these anxieties are not really so modern at all. Perhaps they have always been part of the human condition. Biologist Lewis Thomas wrote, "We are, perhaps, uniquely among the world's creatures, the worrying animal. We worry away our lives, fearing the future, discontent with the present, unable to take in the idea of dying, unable to sit still." This is why Jesus nearly 2000 years ago devoted a large part of the majestic Sermon on the Mount to the affliction of anxiety. And that is why these words have remained etched in the hearts of a hundred generations:

> *"Be not anxious, about your life: what you shall eat… what you shall put on. See the birds of the air they neither sow nor reap, yet your heavenly Father feeds them. Consider the lilies of the field, they neither toil nor spin, yet even Solomon in all his glory was not clothed like one of these. If God so clothes the grasses of the fields which are here today and burned tomorrow, shall he not clothe you, O you of little faith? …Don't be anxious about tomorrow. Let tomorrow be anxious for itself. Let the day's trouble be sufficient to the day."*

Once again, one of the best commentaries on this passage comes from Brother Lawrence, who joined the French Carmelite order in 1666 as a lay brother and whose career was mostly devoted to working in the monastery kitchen. His short and simple meditations "The Practice of the Presence of God" have become a devotional classic. Brother Lawrence writes:

> *"God has infinite treasure to bestow… Blind as we are, we hinder God and stop the current of His graces. But when He finds a soul penetrated with a lively faith, He pours in it his graces and his favors plentifully; there they flow like a torrent which after being forcibly stopped against its ordinary course, when it has found a passage, spreads itself with impetuosity and abundance."*

Brother Lawrence is reminding me that when I do not feel grace flowing through my life, it is not because grace is not flowing. It is simply flowing elsewhere: like to the birds and the lilies and the grasses. I do not feel it because I have little faith in it. Being of little faith stops the current of grace, leaving me anxious and worried. Unfortunately I am often my own worst enemy in matters of faith and grace. As a man who has life-long experience in being his own worst enemy, let me tell you what I mean about how we stop up grace and start up anxiety.

We stop grace when we try to take control of how, where, and when it will flow. We want to change the course of mighty and ancient rivers to fit our personal plans and meet our needs as we imagine them, without seeking out Nature's plans first. We want to change the weather to fit our vacation schedule. We are not satisfied with the way Nature is managing Providence and we think we can manage it better ourselves. Think of 'Retired Executive Syndrome' whereby a man moves to a new town and church, say on the coast of Maine, and thinks how much better he could run things; then sets out to change them into something like the town and church he so eagerly left behind, much to the dismay of all concerned.

We stop the flow of grace when we start thinking that we can earn grace or do something to deserve it or make it happen. This gets us into endless trouble toting up score sheets of all the good things we have done [and just by the way noting all the bad things others have done] trying to get more do-gooder points so the grace will flow to us, us, us. We rush around in our earnest good will being ever more saintly until we are tripping over other equally earnest and saintly do-gooders until we are uttering vile curses at them under our breath. We try to do more and more good deeds until we find ourselves like a Boy Scout helping a struggling old lady across the street, only to find out that she didn't want to cross the street at all, but was waiting there on the corner for her husband to pick her up.

We stop grace when we become anxious that grace will not flow, as if it were up to us to make it flow. This is a little like being afraid that the tide won't come in if we don't check our tide charts regularly. Like the tide, grace flows. It's a law of Nature. It's like 'chi' in Eastern thought. It's out of our hands. But anxiety and fear can stop the flow of grace to us by closing the 'chakras' of faith which allow divine providence to pour in and sustain all creatures from ravens to lilies. Grace flows through us when we open the gates of faith.

We stop the flow of grace when we expect it to come the same way every time. Like a river which cuts a new channel, grace comes in different ways. The way it comes in Boston or Baltimore may not be the way it comes in Blue Hill. The way it came last week may not be the way it will come this week. What worked gracefully in 1972 may not work this year.

There is an old proverb about grace that goes something like this: "When grace does not come early, it comes late. When it does not come quickly, it comes slowly. When it does not come today, it comes tomorrow. When it does not come from above, it comes from below. When it does not come straight, it comes crooked. When it does not come whole, it comes broken. But it comes."

We stop grace when we try to hold onto it instead of letting it flow. If grace does not flow on through us, it will quickly spoil. By a natural process it will decay and become stagnant, thick, corrosive and toxic. Grace is like manna, it only keeps for a day, so you have to go out and get it fresh every morning, and then you have to pass it on. And if you're looking for it, it will be there. The old gospel song goes, "He may not come when you call Him, but He's right on time."

Summer is a most glorious time. The currents of grace flow freely. They flow through the green tissues of trees and the grasses of the field and vegetables in our gardens, making for a soul-stirring beauty and juicy vegetables and fruits to enjoy. They flow through the brooks and streams and through the changing tidal currents of the bays drawing up to the clouds and raining back to the earth. They flow through the laughter of children on the beach and backyard cookouts and campouts in the Maine woods. They flow in rich and poor, old and young. They are the free gift of grace for all creatures. So, let's go with the flow.

Falling Feathers

*Ask the beasts and they will teach you, the birds of the air
and they will tell you, or the plants of the earth, and they will teach
you and the fish of the sea will declare to you. Who among all these
does not know that the hand of the Lord has done this?*

FROM THE BOOK OF JOB

RAMBLERS AROUND TOWN or along the shore these days soon discover fallen feathers of crows or gulls or other fowls of the air; gifts from the sky. This is molting season for adult avians, the time when old feathers are replaced by new, usually after brooding and while food is still abundant. If you are like me, it is hard to pass up a recently dropped feather; it is an exquisite treasure of natural design and construction begging to be taken home. Note, however, that some feathers may not be collected according to the Migratory Bird Act. It might be good to check. Our fire chief and gifted amateur bird carver, Denny Robertson, was marveling the other day about the immensely complicated structure of even the simplest feather. Not only do they have a stem and veins like a leaf, but each vein has feathery edges, too, so that they lock together in flight. On owls the leading edges of the wing feathers are soft and downy allowing them to fly in silence. Ducks and sea birds have an oil gland which helps them groom their feathers so water rolls off like a duck's back. A fallen feather taken home becomes a talisman tying us in with the rest of Creation. Native people have used feathers for ornamentation for millennia. So did Victorian ladies, and even my mother's generation wore feathery hats to church or traveling, though they didn't molt all that much.

While adult birds are shedding the young are fledging. We've been watching a crow's nest in the big sugar maple behind the town hall for a couple of months now; the adults faithfully feeding their fledglings for weeks on end. Then, the end of their labors drew near; it was time for flying lessons in the orchard. Awkward, squawking youngsters bumbled about trying out their new feathers, still white at the base. Flapping frantically they careened from the oak tree into the branches of a lilac bush, then blundered into an apple tree groaning and griping but obviously elated, while the parents cawed their encouragement. Meanwhile, down behind the dam on the mill brook, fledgling mallards paddled along behind their mothers preening and looking over their shoulders admiring their fluffy new coats.

While the birds of the air are earning their wings, the beasts of the field and forest are sending their young forth to an uncertain future. It's heart-breaking to see how many young mammals become road-kill, though we know that far more survive. If you hit an animal or see one in the road, couldn't you stop and put it off to the side in the long grass if it is dead? If it is alive and might survive, contact your nearest animal rehabilitator. If it must be put out of its misery, a sharp blow to the head may suffice as the ultimate act of mercy. Then you will become a member of the order of St Francis who ministered to the birds and the beasts, and they all will honor you.

We are slowly rediscovering and remembering what the ancients knew well—that every creature is kin. We have relatives wherever we look and wherever we go. We never need be alone or lonely again. We are daily invited to one great, wild family reunion. All we have to do is say yes to the invitation, and start getting to know everyone again.

FROM BERND HEINRICH:
We are social animals. We like to feel a part of something of beauty and power that transcends our insignificance. It can be a religion, a political party, a ball club. Why not also Nature?

AND FROM ANNIE DILLARD:
We are here to witness the creation and to abet it.

Family Reunion

*I was suddenly sensible of such sweet and beneficent society in
Nature, in every sight and sound around my house, an infinite
and unaccountable friendliness all at once like an atmosphere
sustaining me, as made the fancied advantages of human
neighborhood insignificant. Every little pine needle swelled with
sympathy and befriended me.*

HENRY DAVID THOREAU 1817-1862

EVERYTHING IS GETTING a little rusty out there as Summer winds
down and Fall comes nearer each day. Leaves on sugar maples are
showing some rusty orange, flower blossoms are tarnished, and
grass is slowly corroding to a silky brown.

At our Cobscook Bay camp your commentator was busy doing
research on young bones, old rocks, older stars and the underside
of clouds, as well as culinary experiments like finding one more
way to serve up a can of sardines. With no phone or electricity or
human companionship this solitude could well have been a sure
recipe for loneliness, but it was not. Blue jays and ravens chattered,
sea ducks flocked and flapped, chipmunks chirped, asters smiled at
the sun and a huge furry yellow caterpillar with black tufts ambled
along the deck happily stopping to taste every fallen leaf its huge
black eyes could see. Believe me, I've been far, far lonelier at a high
school dance, a conference, or a cocktail party. That's because, as
tribal people have known for eons and geneticists are just rediscovering today, all these creatures are also my true and real relatives.
I was at a family reunion in the woods by the shore. All the crazy
cousins were there—not in a hurry, not anxious, not afraid, not
lonely—just content to go about their business without ambition or fear, and happy to let me do the same. Did we talk to each
other? Of course we did. One dark night long before dawn, I was
awakened by the shrill, soaring howls of coyotes very close by and

the answering chanting hoots of loons out on the bay in antiphonal response.

Loneliness is one of the great and primal fears of our species, perhaps because we may be the most self-conscious of any creature. The song of the human ego is "Me-me-me-me-me-me-me;" and when they hear that song, all our four-legged and six-legged, finned and feathered and flowered relatives turn and get out of the way as we go stomping through the tulips. Our little ego wants to be ruler of the world, and, as the saying goes, it's awfully lonely at the top. That's the sad thing about selfishness. The Self always wants to stay up on its high horse alone and lonely above the crowd, while the Heart, the Soul and the Body want to get down, make friends and party with every other cousin creature in the universe, from coyotes to caterpillars. The smallest child knows this and will treat a moth or a mouse as kindly as a man.

If we're ever feeling lonely, all we need to do is get down off our high horse and go outside where there is a perpetual party going on. If we live, we live surrounded by the family of Creation. If we die, we die with that vast family close by on every side. But whether we live or whether we die, we belong to the family of all life: never forgotten, never friendless, never ignored, never alone, always at home.

That's what the yellow caterpillar told me that day on Cobscook Bay.

AUTUMN

The moon is full, the autumn nights grow longer, in the northforests startled crows cry out. Still high overhead, the star river stretches, the Dipper's handle set to southwest. The cold cricket grieves deep in the chambers, of the notes of sweet birds, none remain. Then one evening gusts of autumn come. One who sleeps alone thinks fondly on thick quilts. Past loves are a thousand miles farther each day, blocked from my drifting and my sinking. Man's life is not as the grass and trees, still the season's changes can stir the heart.

WEI YING WU 737-792 AD

SHEEP FROM CARDING BROOK FARM were on our little pasture for a couple of weeks and we got quite neighborly. We gave them drops from our apple tree, and they came a'running whenever we came out the kitchen door. Their sentinel Shy, an elderly draft horse, likes apples too but she prefers eating them out of hand. They're family now. This past week neighbor Jon Ellsworth and I went to his sawmill up in the woods to mill out some roof boards for the shop his son Walker is building for me. Every so often when the saw was quiet we'd hear a soft whirring sound and a huge sawyer beetle would land on one of the new boards or on someone's hat or shoulder. The sawyer beetle gets its name from its fondness for sawmills. Or maybe from the "scritch-scritch" sound its larvae make under the bark. This bug is black with white spots, can grow up to two inches long, and is not so chummy as crickets. Sawyer larvae can do a good deal of damage to diseased or damaged pine, spruce and fir trees that might otherwise make decent lumber. It can also give you a memorable bite. I know because I have been bitten by sawyer beetles more than once. Maybe they mistook me for a diseased pine tree.

Crickets are far more benign. The cricket on the hearth is a universal symbol of domestic comfort and security from China in the East to Europe in the West; and it has been so for thousands of years. Perhaps this is because crickets flourish in open fields and long grass. Where there are open fields and long grass, there are grazing animals; and where there are grazing animals, there is food for omnivorous upright social primates like ourselves. Add a warm hearth with a cricket chirping on it and you have the very picture of domestic comfort and security. This symbolism is captured in homey cricket pillow covers, cast iron cricket boot-jacks, ceramic crickets for the fireplace mantel, and story books and cricket cages for the children.

Crickets have been kept as pets around the world since time immemorial to bring delight with their cheerful songs. In China they are bred to fight. In other countries they are raised by the ton as fish bait and bird food, even human food. Mowing the grass takes a lot longer these days because I try to avoid the hundreds of crickets fleeing in every direction from the snarling mower. I am sure I have killed many, and it pains me, not to mention the bad luck. It is said that you can tell the temperature in degrees Fahrenheit by count-ing the cricket chirps in 15 seconds and adding 37. The feeling of walking through the garden on a sunny autumn afternoon or going out on a starry Fall evening and hearing the singing crickets is joy and contentment. The sound of fewer and fewer cricket calls as the weather gets colder is sadness and nostalgia for Summer past.

In some cultures, crickets are omens of good luck; in others they bring bad luck. Around here, these tiny ebony fiddlers are omens of the end of a splendid Summer season with juicy fruit and lush vegetables from the garden, with visits to the woods and the shore with family and friends; and we hurt to see such a Summer pass. We don't know if the cricket foresees its own fate, but the cheerful cricket on the hearth tells us chances are good that we may yet see another Summer like this gem now ending.

HSIAO KANG 6TH CENTURY AD:
Green leaves that dawn after dawn grow yellow, red cheeks that fade with passing days. If our world is made up of such changes as these, is it strange that my heart is so sad?

A Dangerous Family

THERE IS A DEBATE raging in churches all over America today on the whole matter of faith and wealth. Many churches have taken up the "Prosperity Gospel" that personal wealth is a sign of God's favor. One is Lakewood Church in Houston lately led by mega-pastor and best-selling author, Joel Osteen, who preaches that "one of God's top priorities is to shower blessings on Christians in this lifetime—and the corollary assumption is that one of the worst things a person can do is to expect anything less." Three of the four biggest churches in the country preach the Prosperity Gospel, and hundreds of others incorporate aspects of it. Naturally, they all claim the Bible backs them up.

So, what did Jesus actually say about wealth and poverty?

To answer that let's take a brief look not only at Jesus himself, but his mother, father, aunt, uncle, cousin, and brother who made up one of the most remarkable, and dangerous, families ever seen in history or legend. They represented a revolutionary overturning of the ancient conviction that wealth was a sign of God's favor, and poverty a sign of God's condemnation. They turned the old, weary world upside down.

As the story goes, Mary was a pregnant, unmarried teenager who sang, "God has put down the mighty, he has filled the hungry with good things and sent the rich away empty-handed." Her fiancé Joseph stayed by her and helped raise the son, not his own, teaching him the trade of carpentry, a trade not known for making a man wealthy, as any carpenter will tell you.

Then there was Mary's cousin Elizabeth who ecstatically cried out "Blessed are you among women" when she heard that Mary was pregnant. Elizabeth was married to Zechariah, a quiet, devout man who had a menial job at the temple, also a sure ticket to a life of poverty. Elizabeth and Zechariah's only son, John the Baptist, was a second cousin to Jesus and preached "He who has two coats, let him share with him who has none, and he who has food, let him do likewise." John was imprisoned without trial and executed by the Roman puppet governor Herod for publicly condemning Herod's immorality.

Jesus the son of Mary and Joseph preached, "Blessed are you poor, for yours is the kingdom of God... But woe to you that are rich, for you have received your consolation." Jesus told the rich young man that he lacked one thing. "Sell what you have and give it to the poor," he said, "for it is harder for a rich man to enter into the kingdom of heaven than for a camel to go through the eye of a needle.... Lay not up for yourselves treasures on earth... For you cannot serve God and Mammon." Jesus, as we all know, was executed by the authorities of the Roman colonial government with the consent of the religious establishment after a mock trial.

Then, there was James who was also the son of Mary and Joseph and brother to Jesus according to tradition. In the Letter of James we hear resounding echoes of his brother's preaching.

"Let the lowly brother boast in his exaltation, and the rich in his humiliation, because like the flower of the field he will pass away."

"Listen, my beloved... Has not God chosen those who are poor in the world to be rich in faith... But you have dishonored the poor man. Is it not the rich who oppress you? Is it not they who drag you into court?"

"Come now, you rich, weep and howl for the miseries that are coming upon you. Your riches have rotted and your garments are moth-eaten. Your gold and silver have rusted, and their rust will be evidence against you and will eat your flesh like fire."

James the brother of Jesus was assassinated by the religious elite, the scribes and the Pharisees.

The fierce vision of this remarkable family, which shaped the entire New Testament, left little wiggle room on the matter of riches. An entirely new view of wealth was presented, and an evolutionary breakthrough in human consciousness. In the gospels, riches were no longer the sign of God's favor as in former times, but a major liability in the kingdom of heaven.

Fast forward to today: Government studies indicate that 17% of children nationwide were experiencing food insecurity in 2017, meaning that there are times when they have not had enough to eat or that they did not know where their next meal was coming from. Further news from Washington indicates that for most of the population, there has been no economic recovery. Any improvement has been largely for the wealthiest. And yet, the president's suggested federal budget for 2020 would cut food stamps further.

A while back, I got a call from a woman who lives in her Jeep with her two dogs who are her only family. She works but has no place to stay. The homeless shelter has a waiting list and does not take pets. I got a call from an elderly, disabled man living on Social Security with no car whose food stamps were cut almost 80%. Earlier it was a family with two adults and two children living in a Winnebago in North Blue Hill. These stories go on and on.

The Lord said to Amos, "Hear this, you who trample upon the needy and bring to ruin the poor of the land... The Lord has sworn, surely I will never forget any of their deeds..."

There is a temptation here for some of us middle class do-gooder types to be outraged or infuriated at the greed and obliviousness of the rich and those who cater to them, and maybe feel a little smug and superior ourselves. As satisfying as it might feel to vent our spleen, this helps no one. Many of the super-wealthy are giving generously, others are living in their own hell because more money and stuff can't heal the soul or make one happier, yet they are still craving for money and stuff.

As for us most of us who are neither poor nor very wealthy, the need is so great that the empathetic soul may feel someone else's suffering or need even more than his or her own. He may do everything he can do to help others and find that little has changed, that hunger and suffering and greed and selfishness have not been eliminated from the earth. She may lose heart or hope or just finally burn out and turn away to rest and renew for a while. So be it. The farmer can best tend to his own fields; he cannot tend everyone's. The shepherdess can best tend her own flock, not all flocks. The mother can best care for her own children; she cannot take care of every child in the world or even in her hometown. As with all caretaking, there is always much to do and it will never be all done. Now and then even an angel must fold its wings and rest. At the end of the day even the most righteous must stop and sleep. At the end of the week, even the most holy take a day or two off to give thanks to the One who cares for us all. At the end of a lifetime, our burden will be set down. And rest assured, the burden we set down someone else will take up.

What is needed here is so simple that a child can understand it, and a lot of children do. What is needed is a decent standard of living for every American and for every human. I don't imagine it matters very much to the Lord whether this comes through government programs, or through private charity and philanthropy, or by the blood, sweat and tears of millions of devoted do-gooders laboring at food pantries or soup kitchens or dropping off a basket at a neighbor's, just so long as it gets done. The best case would be if all parties—government, charities, and individuals—agreed that we should have no more hungry, helpless and hopeless children and set out together to make it happen.

One final point: Does that mean there will be no poor in the kingdom of heaven? Jesus said, "The poor you will always have with you" and "blessed are the poor, for theirs is the kingdom of heaven." Here's how I picture it: I imagine *everyone* being poor in the Kingdom of Heaven; not hungry, not ill-clothed, not homeless, not trampled upon, just simply poor by today's standards, but also sharing with each other, caring for each other, working, playing, laughing and singing together, the kingdom of heaven on earth.

What could be richer than that?

POPE FRANCIS:
These days there is a lot of poverty in the world, and that's a scandal when we have so many riches and resources to give to everyone. We all have to think about how we can become a little poorer.

Gathering In

*On such October days as this, we look about us as though in
some new and magic land. The mystical draws close behind
the luminous veil. We see the things about us and sense larger
meanings just beyond our grasp. Looking back on such a time,
we add—as Thoreau did one autumn day—"And something
more I saw which cannot easily be described."*

EDWIN WAY TEALE 1899-1980

THE ANNUAL AUTUMNAL INGATHERING is underway whereby the
yield of Summer is brought in and stored for leaner times ahead.
The last cutting of hay is baled and in the barn. Apple pickers
work their way through the orchards on pointed ladders, bringing in the fruit. Kitchens are fragrant with canning of jams, jellies,
applesauce, pickles and those magical dilly beans that can heal
any malady. Firewood is stacked in the woodshed and the prudent
homeowner begins buttoning up the home. After a couple of hard
frosts have killed the vines, pumpkins are carried from the garden
adding a splash of orange on the front stoop or around the mail-
box out by the road. With every full canning jar, every bushel of
apples, every cord of wood put up our hearts are filled a little more,
leaving less room for the fear of the cold and dark ahead. A full
woodshed and a full pantry make for a full heart, and a full heart
makes for generosity and charity for others.

It is not just humans who are gathering-in these days. The
changing color of leaves signals the gathering of sugars to hardwood roots where it will stay until early Spring. Squirrels and blue
jays gather acorns to be stored in the ground, in a hollow tree, in
a stone wall or an empty birdhouse. It is said that a blue jay can
remember where it has stored thousands of acorns, and the ones it
forgets become the forests of tomorrow. Sphinx moths dart from
flower to flower gathering nectar to sustain them a while longer.

Orange and black ladybug beetles fly the colors of October as they gather on the warm side of the house on these Fall afternoons. We observed another October gathering-in this past week, rather more gothic, when a large female orb-weaver spider and a much smaller male engaged in a Kabuki-like mating dance which ended with the male wrapped tightly in silk to be devoured later by its mate for the purpose of strengthening her to lay eggs. Some of those eggs will survive the coming Winter carrying the genetic memory of generations with them into next year, both spiders dying so that their offspring can live.

October is a month of gathering-in, but also a month of leave-taking and dying. When a soldier or firefighter or crusader for human rights dies in the line of duty, we view them as heroes, sacrificing their lives for others—and that is as it should be, for they are heroes. But, in the end, we all die so that others might live. All of us— from sugar maples, to sparrows, to spiders, to squirrels to spruces, to us— are created to labor in life to make it better for those who come after us, until we die and fly through the luminous veil.

MARY OLIVER 1935-2019:
Don't you imagine the leaves dream now/ how comfortable it will be to touch/ the earth instead of the/ nothingness of the air and the endless/ freshets of wind? And don't you think/ the trees, especially those with/ mossy hollows, are beginning to look for/ the birds that will come—six, a dozen—to sleep/ inside their bodies?

Only a Tramp

HERE'S THE STORY of the rich man and Lazarus, a story that has challenged, mystified, and fascinated scholars for nearly 2000 years. The story goes something like this:

A rich man Dives lived in splendor with purple and fine linen and sumptuous food, while outside a beggar Lazarus lay dying at his doorstep starving and covered with sores. Lazarus asked for some food that would be fed to the dogs, but instead the dogs came and licked his sores. Both men died, as we all do. Lazarus was flown to the bosom of Abraham while Dives descended to Hades where he was tormented in the flames. Dives called out to Father Abraham to send Lazarus with some water to cool his tongue, but Abraham said, "You received your good things in life, and besides, a great chasm has been fixed between here and there that none can cross." Dives answered, "Then send Lazarus to my five brothers to warn them so that they will repent." Then Abraham answered, "They have Moses and the prophets. Let them hear them. If they do not, they surely won't be convinced if someone should rise from the dead."

I said that this story is challenging, fascinating and mysterious. We'll get to challenging in a moment, but let's start with fascinating and mysterious. As you know, much of the material in the gospels is repeated in variations in two or three or even all four of them, or echoed somewhere in the Old Testament. So the first thing that strikes the student of the gospels about the story of the rich man and Lazarus is that it appears nowhere else—not in any of the books of the Hebrew Bible and not in any of the other gospels. It stands alone.

Another fascination of this story is that it lifts the veil of death and describes the life hereafter as few other Biblical stories do. And who has not wanted a glimpse behind that veil? After a lifetime of suffering, Lazarus goes to the bosom of Abraham, a very Jewish scenario of the afterlife. But Dives goes to Hades which is the Greco-Roman underworld. So we have two different ethnic versions of the hereafter side by side. There are many possible sub-texts here beyond the obvious one of the dangers of ignoring the hungry and helpless. There is a suggestion in this parable that the Jews, hungry and oppressed in their occupied homeland, are the righteous, and the Greco-Roman occupiers who oppress them are doomed to Hades. For more on this, read the best-selling biography of Jesus: *Zealot* by Reza Aslan.

However that may be, along with the Good Samaritan and the Prodigal Son – also from the great storyteller, Luke – this story has been among the most told and retold and celebrated in art and song for two millennia, and is far from forgotten to the present day. It appears in 16th century English ballads, 19th century African American spirituals, and 20th century pieces by Benjamin Britten and R. Vaughn Williams, among many others.

The story of the rich man and Lazarus is echoed in a country song "Tramp on the Street" adapted by Grady and Hazel Cole from a 19th century Victorian ballad and performed by countless artists from Hank Williams to Peter Paul and Mary, some of whom added new verses.

> *Only a tramp was Lazarus that day,*
> *He who lay down by the rich man's gate.*
> *Begged for some crumbs from the rich man to eat*
> *But they left him to die, like a tramp on the street.*

Like Christ himself, this is a story that will not die. And that brings us to the challenges of this story, because it is the challenges to our human nature and our habits and daily lives that have kept the story alive.

There used to be a man who often walked through Blue Hill and hitchhiked along Main Street and on out of town. I knew his name and his story. I had known him for years, talked with him often, and gave assistance when it was needed. With his history, believe me, it was a miracle that this man survived at all, but somehow he did, though he was badly broken. And I must confess that there were a few times when I changed my course if I saw him coming. There were a few times when I was relieved that he was on his side of the street and I was on mine, like the priest and the Levite passing by on the other side. There were times when I was happy that a chasm was fixed between us. And in the end, he did not survive his battles.

There are too many who struggle the way he did. And it is up to us to bridge the chasm between us. The great chasm fixed between rich and poor in this state, this country and the world is undeniable, and growing wider every day. And who creates this great chasm? Does God? Or Father Abraham? Or Nature? Or biology? No. We do whenever we pass by on the other side. We do, whenever we think that we deserve what we have and the desperate deserve what they have, whenever we bow to the greedy and congratulate and emulate the super-rich, whenever we feel sorry for the hungry or patronize them instead of giving them what they need to keep them well. We create this chasm. The letter of James reads: "If a brother or sister is ill-clad and in lack of daily food, and one of you says to them, 'Go in peace, be warmed and filled,' without giving then the things needed, what does it profit? So, faith by itself if it has no works is dead."

Will this chasm between rich and poor that we have created determine whether we will spend eternity with Lazarus or with Dives? I'm a theological liberal, you know, not all that comfortable with judgments about the hereafter. But Jesus is unequivocal about it. "'Truly I say to you, as you did it not to one of the least of these, you did it not to me. And they will go away into eternal punishment...'"

Our tradition is unequivocal about the danger of riches to people and nations. The chasm between rich and poor endangers the bodies of the poor and the souls of the rich. It endangers the very survival of our nation, because "a house divided against itself cannot stand, and every kingdom divided against itself will be laid waste."

As mentioned above, I don't imagine it matters very much to the Lord whether this goal is achieved through government programs, private philanthropy, or by the blood, sweat and tears of millions of do-gooders at food pantries or soup kitchens, just so long as it gets done. And if you happen to wake up feeling hopeless, a couple of hours at the food pantry or soup kitchen can be a sure cure. Nothing restores hope like giving someone else hope.

Just as we created this chasm, we can close it. Our tradition is clear on this too. Someone asked Jesus, "Who is my neighbor?" and Jesus told the story of the Good Samaritan. We bridge the chasm when we treat the beaten man not as a stranger, but as our brother and our son and our neighbor, whenever we treat the poor woman not as a point on a graph, but as our mother, our sister, our daughter, whenever we treat the hungry child not as a statistic, but as some mother's darling, some mother's son. We bridge the chasm when we hear Moses and the prophets, when we hear the one who was raised from the dead, when we hear the cries of the beaten, poor and hungry, in Maine, in our country and throughout the earth.

Imagine

*O, lovely raw red wild autumn turning, it's time to think
of the blood, the red searing. Who's there? What's that?
O, to survive what must we do to believe? In the trees, my
grandson. In these roots. In these leaves.*

DOROTHY LIVESAY 1909-1996

FEELING AT HOME in Nature means knowing her with the heart.
Because there are beautiful sights on earth that you and I will never
see. There are enchanting and curious sounds that you and I will
never hear. Smells and tastes abound that you and I can only imagine; textures are everywhere that we will never feel. Being among
the largest of animals [the average is closer to the size of a fly],
our senses are too gross to notice most of the ordinary sensory
events on earth. We depend more on manipulation and thinking
for our survival than we do on our senses. A dog's sense of smell
is much more acute than ours, and the sense of smell of an ant is
several times that of a dog. The keen eyesight of the hawk, eagle,
and other predators is legendary, as is the hearing of the rabbit and
the bat. In short, despite our vaunted intelligence and cleverness,
we are unable to experience, and so are totally ignorant, of most
of what is going on around us. Our cameras, microphones, micro-
scopes, and other instruments give us little clues and snatches,
moments in time, stopped action; the two or three loudest notes in
a "continuous harmony," but hardly a hint of the whole symphony.
After all, a snapshot of the Tower of London and a recording of the
sound of Big Ben don't make one an expert on the affairs of state
of Great Britain. All this going on that we can't hear see, taste, or
smell is like hearing about a great party and not being invited. It's
enough to make you feel left out.

But never mind that. Imagination comes before knowledge and
fills the gaps. Leonardo da Vinci imagined the helicopter and the

parachute hundreds of years before they were developed. Niels Bohr dreamed the structure of the atom before it was ever seen. If someone can imagine the secret sounds and smells, the unknowable sights, tastes, and touches, then knowing them intimately becomes possible. So, imagine the tiny scraping sound of an ant pulling its antennae through the cleaning hooks on its front legs, and the sensation the ant feels while cleaning these highly sensitive appendages. Imagine the clicking of a cricket's feet on a stone wall and the rustle of its wings as it scrambles between two stones... The sound of a mole sneezing... the minute sliding and scraping of an earthworm working its way through the loam. Imagine the smell of a rabbit's breath, or a hawk's, or the odor of the queen's chamber, of a large and busy ant-hill. Imagine the taste of buffalo or beaver milk; the sound of an aphid sucking a juicy leaf; the feel of a butterfly's wings unfolding as it emerges from the chrysalis; or the sound of sap flowing up and down the tree in tiny rivers. Now imagine something unlike anything you have experienced in memory, but have experienced many times in reality: imagine the sight, sound, smell, taste and feeling of a cell wall stretching and the dividing of its chromosomes and protoplasm as a single cell splits into two new living, moving, shimmering cells.

And then, finally, imagine the sound of someone saying that there is no mystery to life.

MAX PLANCK 1858-1947:
Science cannot solve the ultimate mystery of Nature. And that is because, in the last analysis, we ourselves are a part of the mystery we are trying to solve.

Feeling Sorry for God

GOD MUST HAVE a tough job. Not only does He [and I use the pronoun "he" loosely because God is neither He nor She] …not only does She have to paint the wayside flower and light the evening star and order the winds and waves to obey, not only does He have to send guardian angels to all the helpless, not only does She have to watch her warped and wandering children trash each other and the planet, He has to decide whose prayer to answer, the bride who wants the sun to shine for her wedding, or the farmer who wants rain for his parched crops, the paddler who wants it calm so she can go canoeing or the sailor who wants it breezy so he can race across the water, the snowboarder who wants it cold or the surfer who wants it warm. Whose prayer is God supposed to answer?

In the parable of the heartless judge in Luke, Jesus tells the story of a widow who keeps bothering a judge until he hears her case and shows some heart. Then, Jesus tells his disciples to pray persistently and not lose heart if they do not receive an answer right away and not to take no for an answer to prayer. An unanswered prayer might not mean "No", it might mean "What?" or it might mean "Say that again, I didn't hear you the first five hundred times." So keep praying, even at the risk of wearying God. This is what Jesus is saying in this parable. So that is why I say God must have a tough job, and that's on top of being maybe a little hard-of-hearing.

Liturgical prayer as it is done in worship in the Western tradition has a consistency across nations, cultures, languages and through history. Traditional Christian prayer books are remarkably similar around the world. Some prayers we still use today have been part of the liturgy for nearly 2000 years.

But personal prayer is not like this. If you ask 10 or 100 different people about how they pray you may get 10 or 100 different answers. There may very well be as many styles of personal prayer as there are people.

Safe to say, prayer can be divided into two general types, spoken [or sung] prayer and unspoken or silent prayer. As for spoken prayer, traditionally we were taught that a general prayer included petition, confession, thanksgiving and praise, or, as in the title of Anne Lamott's book, "Help, Thanks, Wow"

Prayers of petition, asking for something for oneself or someone else, can be troublesome. Like the simultaneous prayers of the bride for sun and the farmer for rain. What we might want for ourselves or others, might not be what God or Nature or humanity or Creation wants. That is why Jesus taught us to pray "thy will be done." That is why he prayed before his execution, "Let this cup pass from me, nevertheless, not my will, but thine be done." The danger of asking for particular things is that they may not come to pass, and then we may lose heart and give up on prayer or give up on God.

"When in disgrace with fortune and men's eyes, I all alone beweep my outcast fate, and trouble deaf heaven with my bootless cries…" So writes the Bard in Sonnet 29, demonstrating the pitfalls of praying for what we think we want. Or think of Janis Joplin singing, "O Lord, won't you buy me a Mercedes-Benz?"

Unspoken prayer is quite different. It is not thanking or asking or praising so much as it is simply listening to Spirit, or encountering Spirit, or practicing the presence of God. Meditation is a type of unspoken prayer, although the meditator may have a short prayer or mantra repeated during meditation.

So spoken and unspoken prayer are quite different in form and affect. They have one thing in common, though. They are both ways to connect with God or Spirit or the Holy or however you say it. But unspoken prayer has the added dimension of freeing us from ritual and allowing us to live our whole lives as a prayer.

I know it is possible to live out a whole day as a prayer with each thought and word and action given to God, to be in constant touch with the Divine and allow your life to be guided by Spirit. How liberating it can be to give over living for myself and take over living for God. As Alison Krause sings her prayer, "Take my life and let me be a living prayer, my God, to thee…" It's possible to live ones whole life as a prayer. Many have done it.

I don't know about you, but I have a hard time keeping to a regular prayer ritual. If disaster strikes somewhere or if things are tough for me or for someone else, I will pray regularly and fervently for a while. But then I feel better, I forget, I let it slide. And maybe part of me doesn't want to weary God or trouble heaven with my bootless cries. Pretty soon after that, my life starts getting all bollixed up. I am at sixes and sevens. I can't tie my shoes without getting in trouble. My priorities are out of order and I am running from pillar to post without going anywhere or getting anything done. Worst of all, regardless of what else is happening around me, regardless of how good people are being to me, I am feeling lonely, un-noticed and highly insignificant to the world. I am like the plant that hasn't been watered and cannot grow or thrive or bloom or set fruit. I am all dried up and dying inside. I need some living water. This is when I realize that I stopped praying several days ago. And this is when I start praying again. And, it works. I can tell you that it works.

The parable about the widow and the judge is not just about how to pray and when to pray. There is a very powerful sub-text here that is also telling us not to give up in the struggle for justice. Jesus uses the example of a widow in the first century Near East. In that world and in that time, a widow or any lone woman had virtually no rights under the law. She could not buy or sell property; she could be married or divorced without her consent. She could not plead in court; a man had to plead for her. Actually, things were much like that in this country 100 years ago, and are still like that in many countries today, and we still have a long way to go before women are in possession of full rights and powers comparable to those of men.

So in this parable, the widow is going right up to the judge, outside of court, and begging him, wearying him with her pleas for justice. The judge finally gives in, not because the law requires him to, but to get this aggravating woman out of his face. "Though I have no fear of God and no respect for anyone, yet because this widow keeps bothering me, I will grant her justice, so that she may not wear me out by continually coming…" Another version actually reads, "…so that she may not finally come and slap me in the face."

The world sometimes seems like a desperate place full of hate and greed, ignorance and just plain mean ness. A person can devote a lifetime to praying and working for justice and see little change. People still abuse each other, the strong lord it over the weak, and we often fail in even the smallest efforts to make things right. Jesus, who suffered too, told us always to pray and not to faint, that persistence is good strategy; it does work.

Alas, we are inclined to getting impatient and giving up too soon. The struggle to make slavery illegal lasted for generations, and we hear that there are still millions in slavery. The struggle for women's rights also lasted for generations and the struggle goes on, and many did not live to see it end, but they still troubled heaven ceaselessly with their prayers and persisted in their labors.

We may not live to see the reign of justice on earth, either. But that is no reason not to pray and work without ceasing for that justice. It is our persistent prayers and tireless labor today that will bring that reign of justice tomorrow.

Moon and Stars

You know Orion always comes up sideways.
Throwing a leg up over our fence of mountains,
And rising on his hands, he looks in on me
Busy outdoors by lantern light with something
I should have done by daylight, and indeed
After the ground is frozen, I should have done
Before it froze, and a gust flings a handful
Of waste leaves at my smoky lantern chimney,
To make fun of my way of doing things...

ROBERT FROST 1874-1963

WITH DARK COMING EARLIER and staying later and the Full Hunter's Moon just ahead, we have still dodged a hard frost here along the coast. Crickets chirp cheerfully, though a little more slowly. Grasshoppers cling to the screen door. Western conifer seed bugs, sometimes called "leaf-legged bugs," hang around outside looking for a chance to come in where it's warm. Woolly apple aphids float through the air like tiny snowflakes, showing that even the smallest creatures migrate; in this case, from their Summer places on apple trees to Winter lodgings on American elm. A woolly bear caterpillar munches contently on the geraniums we brought indoors before a recent chilly night. He/she will be ushered outdoors later to spend the Winter under some leaf litter, there to freeze solid, then to pupate in Spring, and then to emerge as a Tiger moth. But for now, Woolly makes a fine pet. Blue jays swoop and call raucously while acorns fall and roll down the street to pile up in the gutters.

Our local Benjamin River ospreys seem to have departed for points South. I think I heard their farewell chirps high overhead last week. So those great dark shadows floating overhead in twos and threes, with slightly upturned wings and pinions that look like fingers, are turkey vultures still waiting for a few more road-kills before they head out on their migration. The trailing clouds of far-off tropical storms have brought rain to parts of the inland that needed a good soaking. Before dawn, there is Orion hanging over the southern horizon until the sky brightens enough to wipe him out. My wife Rebecca and I are sure that O'Ryan is really Irish and it's a fiddle, not a sword he is wielding.

We think of pines and cedars as evergreens, but they are now losing some of their needles and the ground is carpeted with them giving off the spicy smell we love. These are, of course, last year's needles. This year's will stay on through the Winter giving us the comforting sight of green against the white and gray. The Full Hunter's Moon rises Sunday evening.

When Rebecca and I lived on West Erie Street in Chicago, way back in the late 60s, there was a street light right outside our bedroom window that we called the West Erie Moon. We joked about it, but it didn't help our sleeping, and I was tempted more than once to take a few potshots at it. The problem of light pollution has only grown since then, and we commend efforts around the world to save the darkness for the peace of mind and wonderment of heart that it brings. Good to keep a wary eye on anyone who can look at the Milky Way and think that we tiny stargazers are intended to rule the earth, much less the cosmos.

SOJOURNER TRUTH 1797-1883:
Those are the same stars, and that is the same moon, that look down upon your brothers and sisters, and which they see as they look up to them, though they are ever so far away from us and each other.

BOOK OF JOB 6TH C BC:
Can you bind the chains of the Pleiades, or loose the cords of Orion? Can you lead forth the garland of crowns in their season, or can you guide the Bear with its children? Do you know the ordinances of the heavens? Can you establish their rule on earth?

Your Neighbor Is Yourself

THOSE OF US WHO LIVE in small towns know the hard truth that it is sometimes easier to feel love for someone we don't even know —a refugee from Iraq or Syria, a hungry child in South Sudan, a celebrity, or even a lost dog—than it is to love someone who is our actual neighbor right next door or up the road. This may be particularly true when our neighbor puts up a sign for another political party, or gets another barking dog to keep the first one company, or runs loud internal combustion engines every hour of the day or night, or… you name it. There are neighbors that are hard to love.

This passage in which Jesus beautifully sums up the entire Mosaic Law and the teaching of the prophets in two sentences appears in all three of the synoptic gospels: Matthew, Mark, and Luke suggesting that this teaching is both authentic and central to the tradition. "You shall love the Lord thy God with all your heart soul mind and strength. And you shall love your neighbor as yourself." The first sentence is called the *Shema* and is at the heart of Jewish faith, being uttered daily at morning and evening prayers. The second sentence is taken from Leviticus and removes all doubt as to what faith Jesus followed. This statement also clearly echoes teachings from the other great spiritual traditions East and West, all of which have variations on the Golden Rule, similar to this one.

The blessing and the curse of small town life are the same: we know each other's business. The old grapevine carries the news around town. We share each other's good times and bad times, and if there is trouble, people try to help, regardless of whether they go to the same church or vote the same ticket. Food and willing hands appear from everywhere. Coffee cans for donations sit on the counter at the store. Benefit suppers are put on. Like it or not, in a small town you are never alone.

Mostly we like it, that's why we're here. But it can have its trials too. Essayist Carol Bly says, "We know what the blessings of country and small town life are. They don't need reiteration. It is our griefs that want change." And we do have our griefs: gossip, rumor, judging, narrow-mindedness and mean-spiritedness. Of course, it has always been this way, but there are some particularly new causes of small town griefs.

One is that many of our towns are growing and new people are moving in. Imagine how a lifelong resident feels going into the local grocery store she has patronized all her life and being unrecognized by anyone there. Imagine a life-long church member saying, "I don't know anyone there anymore."

Also, the new population has moved mostly from cities and suburbs and may not be acquainted with small town life. They may bring urban and suburban ways with them and expect things to be done here as they were back there. In our town of over 2000, it is a rare town meeting that draws more than about 150. Often instead of supporting already existing institutions—churches, lodges, town committees, school activities, all the things that make towns work—the new population sets up its own institutions—schools, businesses, social activities, segregating itself from its neighbors and rejecting the older ways. This does not go unnoticed by those who have labored to keep existing institutions alive for generations.

Next is declining participation in public activities that once brought together people of different opinions and backgrounds and interests as I mentioned. Much of this is because of changes in lifestyle such as television, computers, email, texting, tweeting, both parents working outside the home, and overscheduled children.

And one more, we have shifted our attention from local to global. Local and regional newspapers are falling away like leaves in October while more and more homes are connected to the Internet. I'll bet that most of us know more about what is happening in New

York or Washington or Beijing than we do about our own town or our capital in Augusta. Without the district court reports in the papers and the delinquent taxpayers list in the town report we'd have nothing left to talk about but the foibles of national celebrities. Here's a quiz: name the following: your selectmen or town manager, state representative, public works commissioner, school superintendent, and everyone on your street.

The danger is that the essentially peaceful and happy relations between neighbors enjoyed here for generations will crumble because instead of meeting and listening to all our neighbors, we are listening only to those who agree with us. If we only talk to town leaders or the school principal when we have a gripe, then why live in a small town? After a while, it is easy to see where this will inevitably lead. It will lead to the breakdown of community life.

This has global as well as local implications. If we, who are largely of the same race, language, ethnic background and religious tradition, are giving up on listening to our neighbors and on our traditional town institutions, how can we tout multi-culturalism or bemoan the dysfunction of our federal government or the wars raging elsewhere? It sounds false. It is false.

Another danger is this: If we spend too much time looking at faraway suffering that we cannot prevent or ease, and too little time easing the suffering that is right at hand, we may conclude that the world is a horrible place and we are helpless to do anything about it. Then we fall into despair and pull even further into our burrows. We give up on our neighbors. We give up on hope. We give up on the world. But, when Archimedes said, "Give me a place to stand, and I can move the world," he was talking about leverage. Our leverage is right here. We stand in this place and by loving our neighbors here, we can move the world. Every act of love here sets up ripples and waves that create movement everywhere.

For all his deep faith, Abraham Lincoln was not a church-goer. He reputedly said, "Whenever a church emblazons over its doors this commandment: 'Love thy neighbor as thyself,' that church I will join with all my heart." That's what a church should be about, not judging or condemning, not a factory of fear, but a small town cottage industry manufacturing compassion for export everywhere.

The greatest miracle is not to walk on water or turn water into wine or raise the dead, but to love God and love our neighbor. Everyone is someone's neighbor. Have you ever noticed how the quickest way to stop being sad yourself is by making someone else happy? Have you ever wondered why calming someone else's fears calms your own? Have you noticed how you can stop feeling lonely by reaching out to someone else, or ease your own pain by comforting someone else? This is the greatest miracle, and it's homemade. We ease our own suffering and the suffering in the world by starting right here and working out. Love your neighbor as yourself, because your neighbor is yourself. There's no other way.

Humble Bumble

No one cares for the humble-bee... Humble he is, but wild,
always in the field, the wood, always by the banks and thickets,
always wild and humming to his flowers.

RICHARD JEFFRIES, 1848-1887

BACK IN JULY at our place on Moose Island I noticed that little bumblebees, were flying in and out of the shop where we keep tools, scrap wood, furniture waiting for repair, and a myriad of other things known and unknown. The bees were coming and going between the sloppy kindling pile and the neatly stacked oak. This made me curious and I began a study of bumblebees. I had thought they were solitary creatures, feeding themselves and sleeping under any handy flower at night; and I admired them for that. My studies revealed that bumblebees are not as social as honeybees, wasps and hornets, but do feed a queen bee through the summer. She lays eggs which hatch into solitary queens who leave the nest in autumn and find a safe place to winter over to start more small colonies the next year, while the whole of this year's tribe dies.

At Moose Island again last week, we were painting the house and enjoying some beautiful early fall weather with cool Canadian air pouring in, a waxing moon, and a million stars shining at night. Back in July the bees, probably *bombus terristris*, came and went from the woodpile only occasionally, but this time it was like rush hour at LaGuardia with departures and arrivals every few seconds. And many of these bees were exceedingly enormous, the C-5As of the insect world. This made for some interesting moments getting wood for the 1905 Glenwood Modern cook stove for those cool nights.

Bumblebees do sting occasionally, as I also learned by experience recently, particularly when their work is disturbed. But their sting is mild compared to bees or wasps. One evening I went out to the shop to split some kindling on the chopping block by the kindling pile. As the axe fell and the kindling flew, the stolid bumblebees maintained their familiar flight pattern, buzzing in and out contentedly and mostly steering clear of me. And when I bent over to pick up the kindling with my hindquarters pointed directly into their approach, several of them flew right between my legs and even bumbled into my butt without the slightest sign of hostility, returning to their course toward the terminal of their queen under the woodpile. When I was painting atop a 28' ladder, one even flew into my ear, bumbled a little, and flew back out.

We have long modeled weapons of war after the most aggressive, belligerent insects that fly swiftly, and inflict great pain. The 'Hornet' was a combat plane; the 'Stinger' is a deadly missile. We also admire their 'busy-as-a-bee' industry and acquisitiveness, laying away far more than they need. This fits with the dated view that more aggressive and acquisitive species will survive and the peaceful and contented will not. In the natural world, however, this is simply not the case. My field studies over the years reveal that bumblebees vastly outnumber more aggressive bees and wasps. On blooming fruit trees and on wild and cultivated flowers, bumblebees outnumbered other pollinators by as much as ten to one over the summer. In addition, the highly social honeybees *apis mellifera* have been decimated country-wide by 'colony collapse disorder.' The unavoidable conclusion is that these more aggressive and acquisitive insects are no more successful than the peaceful and independent bumblebees, and perhaps less so.

Peaceful, humble bumbling has worked exceedingly well for the bumblebees, and for most humans through the ages. Maybe our leaders with their endless wars and ever-larger governments and economies should give it a try.

FROM RALPH WALDO EMERSON:
We are reformers in the spring and summer, but in autumn we stand by the old. Reformers in the morning, conservers at night.

I Once Was Lost

THERE'S AN OLD SAYING, "Even the pope must be shriven" meaning that everyone—no matter how allegedly good or apparently powerful—needs to confess the wrongs they have done, make amends, and be forgiven. The selling of indulgences, little pieces of paper that relieved punishment of sins, sort of like "Get Out of Jail Free" cards, incited the opening volleys of the Protestant Reformation nearly six hundred years ago.

For centuries after in Protestant churches people had to make individual public confession of their particular sins to remain in communion. Think what it might feel like to stand up in front of your neighbors and friends and confess how you stole someone's chicken, or cheated the widow who came into your store, or lusted after your neighbor's wife. Two hundred years ago or so, Jonathan and Dolly Fisher, the minister and his wife, had to explain an awkward matter about some port wine that was intended for communion, if I remember right. This sort of public confession made people think twice before they did such things again, and served to strengthen the moral ties of trust and honesty that bind communities together and allow them to thrive.

Over time this sort of public and particular confession gave way to less rigorous collective confessions of general sins – "doing those things we ought not to have done and not doing those things we ought to have done"—as we find in the Book of Common Prayer, so the pain of personal confession was gone, but so was the gain. Even though it is a fading practice in modern Christianity the need for confession and the benefits of it have not faded. They are rooted deep in the human soul.

Paul Martin writes in *The Christian Century*, "A growing measure of responsible opinion argues convincingly that had religion been doing the job it should have done, psychiatry would never have arisen as a profession. Proponents of this view say that the problem is generally not a guilt complex. The problem is *guilt*. Depression, anxiety, hostility, fear, tension and, in more serious cases, psychosis are really ailments of the conscience—symptoms that result from violating the conscience's promptings and refusing to live honestly and responsibly. On this basis, the only way to have the good life is to live a life that is good."

Today, twelve step programs are so effective that they have restored countless lives brought to the brink of destruction by uncontrolled addiction. We know these steps work, and they could have been taken directly from Psalm 32 and the teachings of Jesus. They include admitting I am powerless, turning my life over to God, making a searching moral inventory, admitting my wrongs, asking God to heal them, and making amends to those I have hurt. There is no better path to forgiveness.

Nature, too, forgives. There is a way in which each season forgives the faults and failures of the one before. If Summer was too dreary, Autumn forgives with warmth and sun. If Winter was too cold, Spring waltzes in with balmy breezes. If Spring is too wet, Summer parches. And so it goes. Nature does not want to hold a grudge. She wants harmony more than discord and balance more than revenge. Wounds heal, blood clots, bones knit themselves back together. Polluted water is drawn by the sun into the vast distillery of the clouds where it is purified to fall as pristine rain.

I remember vividly as a boy in western Oregon passing through the aftermath of the great Tillamook Burn, 355,000 acres of old growth forest consumed in several forest fires between 1933 and 1951 leaving a vast deathly landscape. Within a few years the forest was alive again with small spruce and fir shining green among the towering black snags. How long Nature will continue to heal and forgive our abuses, we don't know, but it is manifestly clear that she wants to do so. And God, being the soul of Nature wants to forgive too.

So how do I know when I might need forgiveness? I need forgiveness if I think I've done nothing wrong. I need forgiveness if I think winning is all that matters. I need forgiveness when I think I was just getting even and they deserved what they got. I need forgiveness when I think it's better to just forget about it and it will all blow over. I need forgiveness when I think I don't need forgiveness.

Forgiveness lets us take off our heavy backpack and muddy boots as after a long hike, and sit down by the fire feeling lighter than we've ever felt. The relief is utter ecstasy. Refusing to forgive or ask forgiveness means carrying that heavy pack and wearing those muddy boots until kingdom come.

One last story: at the age of 63, thirty-four years after he had left the slave trade, John Newton—former libertine and slaver, later celebrated minister and author of "Amazing Grace" – was still troubled. Something was still eating at him. Then, he published *Thoughts Upon the Slave Trade*, describing the horrific conditions of the slave ships he had sailed, and apologized for "a confession, which... comes too late....It will always be a subject of humiliating reflection to me, that I was once an active instrument in a business at which my heart now shudders." Newton then joined English abolitionist William Wilberforce, leader of the Parliamentary campaign to abolish the slave trade, and lived to see the passage of the Slave Trade Act 1807 abolishing that evil trade shortly before his death.

Amazing grace, how sweet the sound that saved a wretch like me.
I once was lost, but now I'm found; was blind, but now I see.

November

The great care with which so many of the Indians utilized
every portion of the carcass of the hunted animal was
an expression, not of economic thrift, but of courtesy and
respect—the religious relationship to the slain.

DOROTHY LEE, ANTHROPOLOGIST 1905-1975

HERE WE ARE at the first week in November and still waiting for
a hard freeze. At this writing the leaves are mostly gone from the
trees, but the grass is green, sunflower seedlings are sprouting
under the bird feeders, Queen Anne's lace is still in bloom and so
are the nasturtiums. It seems to be an unusually warm Autumn
we've been having. We will not, however, try to draw any larger
conclusions from that fact at this time. November also means
deer season with all that entails. Hikers now put on blaze orange,
some willingly, some reluctantly. If hunting season rubs you the
wrong way, here are a few upsides of hunting to consider: Some
of the greatest conservationists have also been hunters. Think
John James Audubon, Teddy Roosevelt and Aldo Leopold, for
examples. Hunters know the woods as few others do, especially
if they have been hunting there all their lives, and they will work
to preserve the wilds. Meat taken by hunting has a lower carbon footprint than meat raised commercially. For every pound
of game, there is a pound of beef or chicken that will not be fed
expensive feed, shipped to the supermarket to be wrapped in plastic, brought home in someone's SUV, and its remains taken to
the dump. Game meat is lean, organic and local, probably much
healthier than store-bought meat. Good hunters have a strong
ethic around wild game which includes a fair chase and a clean
kill, tracking down a wounded animal, sharing meat with those
who are unable to hunt, and loathing bad hunters. It is a spirit of
respect and generosity that marks the traditional hunter. There

are bad hunters, for sure, too many of them. But we wear orange to salute the good hunters.

It was a great year for fruits of all kinds. We have seen apple trees that haven't borne in years just loaded with apples. We have eaten some of the finest peaches a person could imagine grown right here along the coast of Maine. The Concord grape vine at our Moose Island house is loaded with deep purple fruit. On the wild side, we don't have the final figures for Maine's current wild blueberry crop yet, but now that the leaves have fallen we can see a crop of Winterberry *Ilex verticillata*, our American holly, far more abundant than any we have seen in years. These cannot be baked into muffins. They are inedible to us [believe me, I've tried] but birds, especially robins, love them. And folks love them for seasonal decorations. Winterberry goes beautifully with evergreens in those vacant flower boxes, and will keep their vibrant red through the Winter to remind us that the heart of Summer still beats beneath the snow.

Climate change is real. We make this statement without hesitation from personal observation. In the nearly 40 years that we have been watching the elements at our Cobscook cabin we have seen higher tides and stronger storms causing more and more beach erosion, and bringing rockweed farther up the beach and onto the field on lunar high tides. This is not something we only saw second-hand on the internet or in the papers or on television. This is something we have seen first-hand with our own eyes. Likewise, we have witnessed changes in New England winters over the past 50 years. Over the years the pattern has been less get-cold-and-stay-cold and more freeze-thaw-freeze-thaw-freeze-thaw. Last Winter this pattern left a foot-and-a-half of ice by true measure over the back field at our house. Never saw anything like it before. What to do about climate change? We've waited decades for governments and corporations to act; now we must.

ALDO LEOPOLD 1887-1948:
There is always something to hunt. The world teems with creatures, processes and events that are trying to elude you. Every ground is a hunting ground, whether it lies between you and the curbstone, or in those illimitable woods where rolls the Oregon River. The final test of the hunter is whether he is keen to go hunting in a vacant lot.

MARY ANN EVANS, KNOWN AS "GEORGE ELIOT" 1819-1880:
Delicious autumn! My very soul is wedded to it, and if I were a bird, I would fly about the earth seeking the successive autumns.

The End of the World, Again?

EVERY FEW YEARS the latest End-of-the-World-as-We-Know-It fad comes around again, but lately it seems to infect more people each time. Remember Y2K? The end of the Mayan calendar? I won't weigh in on predictions which are still pending at this writing in 2020, other than to say that financial crises, earthquakes, epidemics, pandemics, famines, great fires and wars have always followed upon each other after greater or lesser intervals, and as yet the old world is still turning through the seasons.

Can any mortal predict the future accurately? In what is sometimes called Luke's 'mini-apocalypse' Jesus uses traditional language and metaphor to prophesy the following misfortunes: a coming catastrophe including the appearance of false prophets and messiahs, wars and insurrections, persecutions, the destruction of the temple in Jerusalem, the destruction of the city of Jerusalem itself by the Gentiles, cosmic signs of the end in sea and sky, and at last the coming of the Son of Man on a cloud with power and glory.

The events that Jesus appears to be predicting are significant enough that we can check against the historical record to see just what really happened. And sure enough the historical record shows that, after a period of repression and religious insurrection in Judea, Roman legions under Titus Flavius, son of the emperor Vespasian, stormed the city of Jerusalem in 70 AD with massive bloodshed, then sacked the city and destroyed the Second Temple, built by Herod. The Jewish historian Flavius Josephus was a translator for Titus and eyewitness to the slaughter and wrote the following account:

> Now as soon as the army had no more people to slay or to plunder, because there remained none to be the objects of their fury (for they would not have spared any, had there remained any other work to

be done), [Titus] Caesar gave orders that they should now demolish
the entire city and Temple, but should leave many of the towers
standing…in order to demonstrate to posterity what kind of city it
was, and how well fortified, which the Roman valor had subdued;
but for all the rest of the wall [surrounding Jerusalem], it was
so thoroughly laid even with the ground by those that dug it up
to the foundation, that there was left nothing to make those that
came thither believe it [Jerusalem] had ever been inhabited. This
was the end which Jerusalem came to …a city otherwise of great
magnificence, and of mighty fame among all mankind.

Josephus estimated that over a million people were killed and 97,000 enslaved. This was essentially the beginning of the end of the Jewish nation and homeland until 1947.

How did Jesus do with his prophecy? The appearance of false prophets and messiahs? He got that right. Wars, insurrections and persecutions? Yes. The destruction of the temple in Jerusalem and the destruction of the city of Jerusalem itself by the Gentiles? Yes. Cosmic signs of the end in sea and sky? Not in the historical record. And the coming of the Son of Man on a cloud with power and glory? Not yet. But all in all, it sounds like an amazingly accurate prophecy of actual historical events to come.

But, wait, there are a few problems. For one, it is entirely possible that the gospel of Luke was written *after* the historical event of the destruction of the second temple and the city. In fact, most scholars think Luke was written sometime between 75 and 100 AD and that the words of this prophecy were put into the mouth of Jesus by the author of Luke after the fact [or *ex post facto* since we're doing the Latin].

That said, I still find it very plausible that Jesus could have made such predictions some 40 years before the fact. I'll tell you why. As Reza Aslan makes clear in his best-seller *Zealot, The Life and Times of Jesus of Nazareth* [Random House 2013] Jesus lived in a time of mounting religious unrest and increasing oppression by, and resistance to, the occupying Roman Empire. Surely he could see where this all was headed. After all, look how he himself was executed. What is more, in 586 BC the first temple, built by Solomon, had been similarly destroyed and the city sacked by the Babylonians [another great empire that ended in dust]. This event was burned indelibly into the collective memory of the entire Jewish people. So such predictions as these Jesus made were quite reasonable and hardly hallucinatory given the times.

So, what about our rhetorical questions? Can we predict the future accurately? Does history repeat itself in recognizable patterns? We certainly have seen enough historical empires strut upon the scene—with their heavy taxes, mighty armies, torture, oppression and exploitation—to know the familiar pattern. Babylon, Persia, Egypt, Greece, Rome, The Mongols, Turkey, Britain, France, Germany, Russia, America, and others have all had their time of domination, dividing and conquering, ruthlessly exploiting the many for the benefit of the few all the while claiming to be doing God's will, and then faltering, weakening, diminishing and dying when their time is fulfilled. So yes, there are recognizable historical patterns, and we can predict that empires will rise and then fall at great cost in suffering to many. So what does that mean to us living in a modern imperium, however benign?

It means we have some choices. For one, we can choose to side with the imperialists and warmongers, the ones who believe that the gods justify the few of them to have power over the many, to plunder their resources, to exploit them all—man, woman, and child—with little thought for their well-being and no compassion for their suffering, and when they resist to torture and kill them. Many have chosen to side with the powerful through the ages, and prospered thereby, including the historian Josephus who fought against Rome in the First Jewish War and then turned coat and joined up with them in the destruction of his own people and prospered greatly by it. That is one choice.

For another, we can choose to join the resistance as Jesus did and oppose the encroachments of empire with the last ounce of our strength and the last drop of our blood. We can confront and condemn the cruelty and greed that subjects the many to the debased whims of the selfish few always trying to gather more wealth and power to themselves. We can break the unjust laws that legitimate exploitation and we can take whatever punishment comes. We can stand in front of the tanks and lie down in front of the bull-dozers. We can rot in prison or go to the cross like Jesus.

But you know something? Speaking for myself only here, I am not Jesus. I admire and revere the man, but I could not do what he did. So, I am glad there is another choice available to a follower of Jesus, someone a good deal meeker than he was. That would be to join the peaceful insurrection that is sweeping the country.

While huge, bureaucratic and exploitive economic systems like corporate health care, industrial agriculture, the military/industrial complex, and national government continue to fail, small local efforts are springing up to build a New Jerusalem founded on compassion. Local agriculture, food pantries and soup kitchens and free clinics, alternative practitioners and entrepreneurs of all types, small businesses and cottage industries are rising up to be ready to take the place of the foundering bureaucracies when they fall, as they surely will, with not one stone left upon another. "The meek may inherit the earth," said oil billionaire J Paul Getty, "but not until I'm done with it!" Well, he's dead and he's done with it, and the meek are coming into their inheritance.

Stand up and raise your heads, for your redemption is drawing near.

Thanksgiving

*When you rise in the morning, give thanks for the light,
for your life, for your strength. Give thanks for your
food and for the joy of living. If you see no reason to give
thanks, the fault lies in yourself.*

ATTRIBUTED TO TECUMSEH, SHAWNEE LEADER 1768-1813

IN THE COURSE OF the last quarter moon the colors of the season
have changed. The grass fades to brown and so do the fallen leaves
that were so vibrant in October. The bright flowers of the garden
have lost their brilliant reds, yellows, and oranges and are turning
back to the colors of the earth from which they came and to which
they are going. The angle of the sun throws long shadows that
seem to signal something just beyond our threshold of awareness,
something foreboding. Then, one morning from roof top to tree
top and from fence to fence it is all covered in a universal white
and it is as if we are all transported together to an entirely different country with different clothing and customs and climate as the
prelude to Winter gets underway once again.

There are three working farms in easy walking distance from our
home in Brooklin—Carding Brook, Stoneset, and Poland Family
farms. This offers many benefits including fresh vegetables and
fruits in season, the sounds of roosters crowing, chickens clucking
and cattle lowing, and the sights of great draft horses pulling, goats
climbing stone walls, and little black pigs foraging for acorns under
the oak trees, with a home-made sign beside the road saying on
one side "Beware: Swine Strolling" and on the other side: "Pigs
Patrolling" or something like that. It is traditional in autumn to
let the pigs loose in the woods to feed on "mast," that is, the fallen
nuts of oak, beech, hazel, and others, and the acorn crop, like the
fruit crop, looks to be abundant this year. Those years when the
wild nut crop is heavy are called "mast years" and they are a boon

to squirrels, jays, black bears, foraging pigs, and others. There is apparently evidence that oak trees somehow decide together to all crop heavily in a given year, and your commentator does not want to dispel that beautiful notion of a council of mighty oaks. Nevertheless, a lifetime of tree-watching and caretaking suggests that weather conditions during pollination are the main determining factor for the abundance of the crop, as it is with fruit trees and many other plants.

Tecumseh was a Shawnee leader who lived in very troubled times for his people. And yet, he apparently felt the need to give thanks every day. Perhaps this gives an insight into how Native Americans lived on this continent for millennia without creating any of the major crises we have created. Think about it—while they lived on the continent for at least ten thousand years prior to the arrival of Europeans, all the water was safe to drink, the air was everywhere pure. All meat they ate was free-range and organic, animals were killed with respect and gratitude, and every part was used. All vegetables were local and organic, too, And, by the way, they gave us corn, beans, squash, potatoes, tomatoes, chocolate, peanuts, peppers, pineapples, pumpkins, sweet potatoes, and avocados. Everything they used was made of natural materials and was totally recyclable or compostable. They had no plastic, no trash, no litter and no dumps or landfills. No one was hungry [unless everyone was hungry], and no one was homeless. Status was not measured by how much stuff you had, it was measured by what you did for the tribe. In many cases it was measured by how much you gave away. Giving thanks was central to the Native American way of life, and it still is. It's worth pondering how gratitude enabled them to flourish for so long while avoiding the major crises we now face. It's worth pondering.

   Ultimately, gratitude is a pure matter of survival for all of us. Why?

Gratitude leads to joy, undeniably a healthy exercise. It might seem that joy comes first, then gratitude. But it also works the other way, give thanks, and feel the joy begin.

Gratitude acts out the truth that we are not alone but connected, and that the good which comes to us comes from beyond us, so being thankful overcomes feelings of depression, isolation, and alienation and joins us to the human community, the ecological biosphere, and the Creator of it all.

Gratitude counters abuse and greed. When we are thankful for things, we do not abuse, debase, corrupt or destroy them, or think we 'deserve' them. Gratitude makes us more content with what we have, not always feeling entitled to more, more, more.

Gratitude leads to generosity and compassion. That is why thanksgiving means not just giving thanks; it means giving help. "The thankful receiver," wrote English poet William Blake, "bears a plentiful harvest."

Gratitude cannot be taken away from us against our will. It is an affirmation of life which is always ours to express. No one can stop or restrain or prohibit us from the practice of thankfulness or the enjoyment of its benefits. It matters not how much we have. "I am grateful for what I am and have," wrote Thoreau. "My thanksgiving is perpetual…O how I laugh when I think of my vague indefinite riches. No run on my bank can drain it, for my wealth is not possession but enjoyment."

Yet, there is still one stumbling-block here. We've all known people who practice their Christianity faithfully, worship regularly, support their church, celebrate Thanksgiving, and are still angry, obsessive, vengeful, greedy, or unforgiving, or simply depressed or alienated.

Going through the motions, though it is a start, is not enough. Garrison Keillor remarked, "Going to church will no more make you a Christian than joining the Elks club will make you a large antlered ungulate." To work, the spiritual practice of gratitude must be long-cultivated and deep-rooted in the soil of the soul.

In the end, real gratitude calls for a radical change of attitude. This is the real work, and it is internal work. Tecumseh said, "If you find no reason for giving thanks, the fault lies within yourself." Tough, but true. A thankful heart is a gift that we can give in exchange for all that we have received. Ingratitude closes the gateways of grace. Gratitude opens them.

THOMAS PAINE 1737-1809:
But if objects for gratitude and admiration are our desire, do they not present themselves every hour to our eyes? Do we not see a fair creation prepared to receive us the instant we are born—a world furnished to our hands that cost us nothing? Is it we that light up the sun, that pour down the rain, and fill the earth with abundance? Whether we sleep or whether we wake, the vast machinery of the universe goes on.

WINTER

Making Light of It

Every stump is sacred. Every stump is a saint. Every silted river a church to which the pilgrim salmon return. Every breath of wind is a love song. We worship in wetlands, bow to the fern, the rock, the holy salamander, the blood of sweet water, the body of moss.

MAINE POET GARY LAWLESS

IT'S CURIOUS THAT just now when our Northern skies and lands are becoming darkest, nearly every religion is entering a season of light. The shortest days and longest nights loom in on us, and yet everywhere people are gathering and praising the light. We make fire in our fireplaces, we light candles. We hang evergreen wreathes on our houses and haul green trees into our living rooms now that the green is gone from our fields. We fill our flower boxes with greens and reds. What kind of madness and folly is this?

It is the madness of memory and the folly of hope. The madness of memory is that it is not bound by what the eyes see. It remembers the recurring rhythm of darkness and light and knows that the light always follows the darkness. The folly of hope is that it strengthens and nourishes itself by things not seen. Memory and hope hold the soul above the flood of fear and the deluge of death and say, "No, it shall not be so forever, but only for now. The darkness is just for a time. The light will return."

The evergreens and the candles in the windows are talismans, strange devices that recall to our memory the Great Life and the Great Light, just as the Great Life and the Great Light are receding far away from us out onto the distant rim of the turning year. With these talismans we are united with the ancient people who had no calendars or almanacs, but a deep and wide corporate memory from times even more ancient than their own. It was the recurring pulse of this memory that made them joyfully gather greens and light fires in the deep dark.

With our science and cosmology, our atomic and digital clocks, satellite telescopes and mass spectrometers, our charts and graphs, our core samples of ancient glaciers and ancient trees, we have certainly not lost the memory. With the help of our advanced technologies, we have gathered the data of the past and minutely cataloged it all. In so doing we have retained for ourselves the memory. But in spite of all of its reach and grasp and precision, our science has failed to retain for us the hope.

So, in barns and sheds and kitchens and church basements, we sculpt and craft and manufacture hope with our own hands from the simplest things in the simplest ways, bending boughs of balsam into wheels of life and blending bayberry and beeswax into flames of light. We manufacture life out of death and light out of darkness. Without words or printed pages, we self-publish the good news, a testament of natural things that the light will always shine in the darkness and the darkness will never overcome it.

Apocalyptic Pie

Snowfall, slow fall of so many crystalline pieces;
snowfall of a thousand footsteps; slow, sure descent,
rhythmic it is. Snow falls on everyone equally...
Thoughtful, snow is, as it falls on everyone so equally.

FROM RED HAWK "PIPIKWASS"

A REAL HARD FREEZE came our way this past week, the coldest temperatures since way last Winter. The ground heaved and pushed up spikes of ice crystals which shattered and crunched underfoot walking about on a frosty morning. Puddles froze over and the birdbath became a tiny skating rink, surprising a few finches expecting a drink and getting a slide instead. Smoke rose straight up from chimneys and crows and ravens muttered on snow-laden branches. Deer danced daintily in the new snow. Those of us who retreat to shelter during the cold threw another log on the fire and put the pot on to simmer.

One of the delights of the first snow is that it lays down a parchment upon which the creatures can inscribe their lively motions over the course of the day, a manuscript that can be read and interpreted by the careful observer.

Mix together the longest nights and shortest days of the year, the growing cold and snow, and the usual shenanigans in Washington and you have a mighty fine recipe for apocalyptic pie. "Where is the world going and what are we doing in this hand-basket?" reads the bumper sticker. Those whose minds incline toward the dire are overcome by anxiety. Some say the sky is falling, and that is true. But the sky has been falling since the beginning of time. Rain and snow, sunlight and starlight, cosmic dust and debris, millions of meteorites of carbon and water, all of these pieces of the sky have been falling since the earth was born. And together they make life possible on this blue-green planet. Some say the world is coming to an end and that is true too. The world that goes to sleep at night is never the same world that wakes up in the morning. Mountains rise and fall, deserts drift, rivers change their courses, creatures age and change. Today the sun rises on a new earth and tomorrow it will again.

This is not to deny the reality of the Armageddon now raging in what was once called "the cradle of civilization" where great heartless corporations and nations struggle for control of the lands and resources of others, contemptuous of the inhabitants who want only to live their lives in peace and unafraid. The cataclysmic turmoil and violence in the Middle East, most of it against women and children, is surely the end of *their* world, and it will not go unpunished, as nations and people are judged for their actions in the fullness of time. But it is also true that these are un-natural events perpetrated by overweening human greed and corruption; crimes against all of humanity committed by fewer than 1% of humanity. These are not acts of God, or natural upheavals of the Earth.

Whatever may be the causes of such catastrophes, compassionate souls react in the same way. They are emergency workers of mercy, they are first responders of faith, speaking out loudly against the inhumanity, sending or bringing help to the helpless, welcoming the stranger and the refugee, refusing to keep silent or look the other way.

In this season of mercy and peace, the merciful work for the end of the old world of cruel and heartless men wielding the threat of destruction over all that breathes. The merciful work for the birth of the new world where the needs of women and children come first and the weapons of war and the instruments of greed are thrown on the smoldering trash heap of history.

FROM THE PROPHET ISAIAH C 6TH CENTURY BCE:
The people who walked in darkness have seen a great light; those who dwelt in a land of deep darkness, on them has light shined... For every boot of the tramping warrior in battle tumult, and every garment rolled in blood will be burned as fuel for the fire.

Wheels Within Wheels

As for the appearance of the wheels and their construction: their appearance was like the gleaming of beryl; and the four had the same form, their construction being something like a wheel within a wheel. When they moved, they moved in any of the four directions without veering as they moved.

VISION OF EZEKIEL 6TH CENTURY BCE

THIS TIME OF THE YEAR we are likely to feel that we are being plunged into darkness. On a cloudy Winter day here, nearly half-way to the North Pole, it starts to get dusky around 3:00 in the afternoon and the days are still getting shorter. It is the growing cloak of the darkness and the low angle of the sun that creates this mood. Darkness seeks domination. But the light, as limited as it is, resists, and it has great power too.

The other day as I was going about my business in town an hour before sunset, I caught sight of a bright light in the Western sky, a light that was not the sun. Finding a place where the horizon could be seen without obstructions, the greatest display of solar reflections and refractions I had ever seen suddenly distracted and overwhelmed me. In the Western sky was the muffled glowing disk of the sun like a luminous sphere of cotton hanging an hour above the horizon line of spruce and fir spires. Then as my gaze expanded far outward I saw the storied "circle 'round the sun" with a diameter of scores of suns and tinted with faint rainbow colors. The bottom of the circle was cut off at the horizon but at the right and left, North and South, were two brilliant "sun dogs" or parhelions, mock suns shooting out rainbow hues suspended on the great circle and reflecting the brilliance of their original in the center. These I had seen before a few times in my life. But new wonders awaited.

As my eyes wandered to the top of the great circle, I saw part of another circle just resting on the first, its arc rising into the sky like horns or the points of a crown. But that was not all. Tilting my head back and shouting in jubilation, I opened my eyes to see a circular rainbow at the very apex or zenith of the sky directly overhead, not just an arc, but a complete, entire circle of the full spectrum of all colors floating directly overhead. Never before or since has this poor mortal witnessed such a breath-taking presentation of circles upon circles, wheels within wheels of unimaginable circumference of white and rainbow light painted in the sky from horizon to apex. What a marvel! Like a glimpse of the bone structure of the cosmos, and the bones were made of light.

Lest you think this was a dream, five other people witnessed the same. Yes, we know that this phenomenon can be explained by the presence of ice crystals in the high atmosphere and by the laws of optics and the refraction of light. Just about any miracle can be gutted by a scientific explanation, if one is so inclined. But that will never, never be enough for me.

How to Hijack a Church

*Never doubt that a small group of thoughtful committed citizens
can change the world; indeed it's the only thing that ever has*

ATTRIBUTED TO MARGARET MEAD

LET'S SAY WE ARE LIVING in a town that has seen changes over the
years; and what town hasn't? Let's say we are not particularly inter-
ested in religion—or that we are—and we have noticed that the
little church in town is starting to look run-down. Its paint is peel-
ing, shingles are starting to blow off the roof, and just a few people,
or none, are using the building. According to Gallup, Americans
claiming church membership dropped from 70% in 1999 to 50%
in 2019. What we are seeing are the dry empty husks of institutions which once helped to define our daily lives and our nation.
At the same time, current studies show that 70% of the population
feels lonely and isolated.

Let's say we want to preserve this historic building, or want to
see it come alive again or maybe even become a cultural and spiritual asset to the whole community, instead of an eyesore. There are
more and more of these old buildings that have escaped destruction
by the efforts of small groups of people. Instead of falling down,
or becoming condos, they have become arts centers, non-denomi-
national or even non-Christian places of worship, concert venues,
schools, or community centers. The social gathering/bonding,
long the beating heart of these churches, has been revived. Let's
say we want to make this happen in our town.

What do we do to make this happen? First thing to do is form a
committee, but we don't call it that. We call it a working group or
task force or SWAT team or a coven or anything but a committee.
But we need a group of people who share goals, the first goal being
to see that the building does not fall down.

Most small town churches in New England are Congregational

or Baptist. That likely means that the building is entirely owned by the members, and that they make all the big decisions, generally by majority vote. There are no bishops, no hierarchy to speak of in these churches. [In contrast to Catholic, Episcopal, Lutheran and Methodist churches where the local congregation generally does not own the building.] So if our little church is still active, we can simply join the church together as a group. If the church has five members and our group has six, we are a majority. If the church requires affirming a covenant that some of the group cannot tolerate, maybe they can join as parish members, a traditional type of social membership. Or they can just cross their fingers and affirm the covenant. It's all metaphorical anyway.

As an aside here, small churches are a paradigm for many other human institutions. Just as many historically celebrated musicians, scholars, academics and public figures started out in a local church, so lessons learned in these small community organizations can be applied far beyond our little towns. I'm not going to say that if you can hijack a church, you can hijack a large corporation. But I'm not going to say that you can't, either.

At this point in the game, a plan with set goals is needed. If the building is abandoned, we can go to the town with a plan for rehabilitating it and they might just give it to us. Or perhaps a kindly individual has bought the building, or given it to the historical society. Our plan needs to have short-term goals like fixing the roof, broken windows, faulty plumbing. We also need long-term goals, a dream list, like equipment and staff, and ways to fund these goals like publicity, fund-raising events, potential donors big and small, and crowd-funding. Maybe we want to incorporate non-profit, or maybe we can work under the church's non-profit status. It's amazing once the ball gets rolling how donations and funding appear and volunteers come around.

Locally advertised fundraising events *in the building* are important to get more people inside and comfortable with the place. If there is a rudimentary kitchen, pot-luck dinners are good. If the organ or piano still functions, hymn-sings are good. Coffee-house programs with live local musicians are good, especially if some of the proceeds go to the local food pantry or heating fund. All these also serve the purpose of bringing people together for community activities. Maybe you will put up one of those hokey giant thermometers out front to show fundraising progress. Now you are on your way.

It's good to keep in mind along the way that the old church building will exert an influence of its own on this project. There is a powerful lot of history and spirit permeating those old boards and beams which have absorbed the preaching and prayers, the disputes and the benevolences of a congregation through many years. The building is not simply a lifeless platform on which our schemes and plans will play themselves out just as we imagined. It is a living part of the new endeavor that will take place within its walls and will shape the outcome of our labors in ways we could not imagine at their beginning.

New World to Come

Beneath the winter's chilling snow, the heart of summer beats below;
Beneath the old world you can see there breathes a new world that will be.

TO BE SUNG TO THE TUNE OF TALLIS CANON

INSTEAD OF DISDAINFULLY DISMISSING perpetual forecasts of the end of the world, suppose we were to concede that the old world *is* ending, "not with a bang, but a whimper," as T.S. Eliot put it. After all, it has happened before. The Permian extinction 250 million years ago ended the world for roughly half of all species, marine and terrestrial. The Cretaceous extinction 65 million years ago—from a large meteor strike—ended the world for about one-third of all species. And, of course, orthodox believers will tell you about Noah's flood which wiped out all but a few individuals of every kind when mighty Jehovah got fed-up, sick and tired of mankind's evil ways. That may be history or myth, but there's plenty of evidence that we are in the midst of another cataclysm right now, and darned if mankind's evil ways aren't at the bottom of it again, or so they say. But, don't give up hope. Don't sell all your earthly goods and climb to the top of the mountain one morning early to greet the end of it all.

Why? Because the end of the old world also means the beginning of the new, and that is something to await with anticipation and hope. So what might the coming new world look like? The new world will turn the old world upside down. It will have an economy based on need, not greed. It will give the wants of children priority over the desires of generals. It will give power to the weak, not to the powerful. It will "fill the hungry with good things and send the rich empty away," as sang Mary, the mother of that boy-child. The new world will be first in full accord with the needs of the planet, and not just the needs of the human race. It will treat all lives, not as goods to be bought and sold, but as miracles to be honored and treated with reverence. It will be a world made, not in the image of only one creature, but in the image of the Creator of it all. That new world has been promised from ancient times, and is coming. We can see it, we can hear it, we can feel it now.

FROM WALT WHITMAN
I swear the earth shall surely be complete to him or her who shall be complete; the earth remains jagged and broken only to him or her who remains jagged and broken. I swear there is no greatness or power that does not emulate those of earth; there can be no theory of any account unless it corroborate the theory of the earth. No politics, song, religion, behavior or what not, is of account, unless it compare with the amplitude of the earth.

AND FROM AMERICAN HUMORIST ROBERT QUILLEN 1887-1948:
If we wish to make a new world, we have the material ready. The first one, too, was made out of chaos.

Little Acorns

And in despair I bowed my head:
"There is no peace on earth," I said,
"For hate is strong
and mocks the song
of peace on earth, good will to men."

FROM HENRY WADSWORTH LONGFELLOW 1807-1882

ONCE LONG AGO, a tiny oak tree was planted near a house—too near. After a couple of hundred years, its enormous limbs loomed threateningly high over the fragile roof-beams; and its great roots heaved up the front porch, dislodged the heavy foundation stones and threatened the whole house. I know, because I saw it. It is easy to forget what someday might become of it when we are admiring a tiny smooth brown acorn gently held in the hand.

Christmas is a little like that. It celebrates the birth of a tiny brown babe, sweet and helpless. But this acorn of a baby grew up to be an exceedingly powerful and dangerous man, threatening the established order of his time. According to the oldest traditions, he also sprang from a dangerous family tree. Look at the record.

His mother Mary sang about the mighty being thrown down and the lowly raised up, the poor being filled with good things and the rich being sent away empty. He and his cousin John the Baptist and his brother James preached the golden rule and the meek inheriting the earth. They were revolutionary enough to make the American Adams family look passive in comparison.

Mary, Jesus, John and James, all born into poverty and powerlessness, proclaimed a peaceful pouring out of divine love and justice into the world. They threatened the domains of the orderly immoral, exploitive, and militaristic powers of their time; and these cruel powers struck back with a vengeance. Though they preached and practiced non-violence; these three men were all arrested, tried, tortured, and put to death by secret military tribunals. And yet, the peaceful, revolutionary and divine new order these radical bearded rag-heads envisioned changed the world.

Like great trees, revolutions grow old and die. Again today, the world is ruled by orderly, cruel, immoral, exploitive, and militaristic regimes. But, the seeds of non-violent justice and peace are still being planted today, as this holy family planted them in their time, and others have in other times. There can never be justice without peace, or peace without justice. Never was, never will be. It's a natural law.

This is something for us to ponder in our hearts when we sing softly and sweetly about the Virgin Mary and the holy, homeless infant so tender and mild—it's one dangerous holy family we sing about this season. It's something for us all to ponder in our hearts when many myriads of holy, homeless infants are being born to us today among the millions in Iraq, Afghanistan, Sudan, Syria, the West Bank and Gaza, in Aleppo, in Flint, at Standing Rock, under plastic tarps in world-wide refugee camps, detention centers, reservations, and ghettoes in all the world's great cities... Little acorns. It's something to ponder in our hearts.

G.K. CHESTERTON 1874-1936:
The trouble with Christianity is not that it has been tried and found wanting, but that it has never been tried at all.

AND FROM LONGFELLOW AGAIN:
Then pealed the bells more loud and deep:
"God is not dead, nor doth he sleep; the wrong shall fail, the right prevail, with peace on earth, good will to men.

She Sleeps

WITH EVER-DIVIDING BRANCHES rising from their roots in the earth, the armatures of oaks, maples and birches stand out against the Winter sky like lofty, lifeless species diagrams drawn from a lecture by the Architect of the Universe. A hardwood tree in January looks as dead as can be, but break a maple twig on a warm day and you may quickly notice a faint pulsing of sap and later a tiny icicle hanging from the wound. Take a piece of firewood from the wood box and notice two kinds of growth rings, the wider, lighter, softer Summer rings and the narrower, darker, harder Winter ones. In its deep sleep a tree still slowly grows even in the dead of Winter. It is sustained by the food it made during the leafy months and stored in its roots for the leafless days ahead. In the woods, squirrels and field mice survive on nuts and seeds they gathered before the snow and cached away underground.

Somewhere on the mountain a great mother black bear sleeps the long sleep of Winter in her den, eating nothing, breathing invisibly, heart barely beating, gestating a tiny pair of cubs within her warmth. Imagine her simple hibernal dreams of fresh air and water, sparkling sun, rich browse, and ample nuts and berries. She has nothing, and yet these dreams are enough to sustain her. We have everything, yet never enough to satisfy us.

Aside from always wanting more and not sleeping all that well, we're not so different from the bear really. Our bodies survive the Winter on stored food. And our souls survive on stored dreams tucked away in our hearts on brighter, warmer days. Our souls take nourishment from the thoughts and theories, stories and songs cached in books, plays, concerts and ceremonies. If we manage to grow a little too, it is by feeding on the rich reserves of the past. This growth may be darker and harder like Winter wood, but it gives us a stalwart durability to stand up to storm and cold, and the simple rigors of Winter life.

Just as we store up fuel and food during the warm months to sustain us through the cold, we can store up plans, dreams and visions during the cold months to inspire and guide us when the leaves again return to the trees. It is a time to look back and pack up the past, then look forward to form the future.

Plot out your next garden or book or painting or wedding. Sketch the new boat or the new out-building or the new world. Dream up new schemes to save money or energy or time or the planet. Envision a trip beyond the far corners of your town, or beyond the far corners of your mind. In a warm window, start seeds of broccoli and beauty, cilantro and silence, hollyhocks and hope, cabbage and compassion, peas and peace, to enrich the dreams of a bleak midwinter.

FROM THE OLD FARMER'S ALMANAC 1803:
If men, with minds as cool as the evening, will lay out the work of the day, they will be able, in this leisurely January month, to lay plans for a life of prosperity and happiness.

January Dreams

AFTER A BITTER NEW YEAR cold snap came an early January thaw blowing in from the Southwest. The ice on ponds and lakes turned soft and milky. The mill brook began to gush again, the sheet of ice covering the inner bay began to retreat back towards shore and ice dams came crashing down off the eaves startling the dwellers inside lost in daydreams of castles in the air. Squirrels roused themselves from their Winter sleep to frantically shuck spruce cones for a quick power meal on the mountain or staked out their turf under the bird feeders chasing away all comers down in town. Chickadees added an extra lilt to their melodies and, sure enough, the redpolls came back to the feeders. And, like the other critters, we got busy finishing up chores and outside jobs that were waiting for a break in the weather. All at once, it was quite busy in Awanadjo country. Is it the warming that causes all this running around, or is it the running around that causes all this warming?

It seems that the National Oceanographic and Atmospheric Administration now regularly declares last year to be the warmest year on record. So far. Putting aside the hubristic folly of NOAA's title [who actually administers the oceans and the atmosphere?] it would take the density of granite for anyone to doubt the reality of global warming by this time. Even though hard statistics only go back a century and a half, core samples from deep Arctic ice and old trees show that Earth's climate today is warmer than it has been in a very long time, and getting warmer. True, a warming climate can sometimes be a good thing. A warming period in Europe during the 11th and 12th centuries led to increased production of grain which led to larger and healthier populations and stronger economies which led to the building of magnificent cathedrals, which were the technological equivalent of our putting a man on the moon, and equally elegant, reverent and awe-inspiring. They marked the end of the Dark Ages. These marvels of human engineering still astound us and call us to better things.

Suppose we were to use the present warming to accomplish things equally beautiful and awe-inspiring. What might they be? A great cathedral was a true castle in the air serving as the spiritual and material heart of the surrounding region, calling artists, musicians, merchants, craftsmen and farmers into its sheltering shadow to do what each did best. Goods and food were sold, music and drama were performed, and thanks were given to the Creator of it all. Many of our towns and cities traditionally played a similar role. Missing from the picture today are enough good local food and good local jobs, with the result that moving people and goods from where they are to where they are needed has become the root of so many modern evils, including global warming. We need to be bringing it all back home; producing food and goods where they are needed, and thus bidding farewell to poor food, joblessness and the toxic reek of burning hydrocarbons, while creating zones of beauty and elegance like the cathedrals of old.

FROM HENRY DAVID THOREAU:
If you have built castles in the air, your work need not be lost; that is where they shoul be. Now put the founations under them.

AND FROM MARGARET FULLER:
Men, for the sake of getting a living, forget to live.

Intelligent Evolution

A DEAD LEAF, etched with a pattern like the tree from which it fell, blows along the path. The symmetrical exoskeleton of an insect caught in a spider web trembles in the breeze. The silky seeds of milkweed and thistle trace the wind currents flowing over the mountain. The antlers of a white-tail buck reach up to grasp the sky and the elegant musculature of a doe stretches to leap over a stone wall. All so intelligently evolved to fulfill the lives they lead.

Some people get nervous when they hear talk about 'intelligent design in Nature,' thinking perhaps that someone is trying to sell them a cleverly disguised reissue of an old Biblical God. So they loudly raise the standard of rationality, put on the armor of analysis, and take up the sword of science to attack the 'myths' and 'fuzzy thinking' and 'ignorance' and 'superstition' of honoring any sacred dimension in Nature. They loudly trumpet the call to arms of human intellect soon to vanquish all the unknowns, all the holy mysteries of this vast universe. They bray about the day to come when humans will know everything, and own everything.

Remember, though, any theory that everything emerged from material randomness and mindless chemical interaction gives some distinct competitive advantages to certain parties. This view turns the great living, spinning, roaring, surging, sprouting cosmos into a mechanical or mathematical problem soon to fall to our technology. It tears the soul out of Nature. It drains the Spirit out of life, and it sets up the Mind of Mighty Mankind as the greatest intelligence of all, thereby anointing him as the new Master of the Universe, like Napoleon crowning himself emperor. This view then makes the whole Creation and every creature a natural resource that humans are ordained to use for their own tiny, selfish purposes. This is the theology of artificial intelligence, cloning, genetic engineering, atomic power; of slavery, factory farming and fracking. This is self-idolatry; this is folly, and the road to madness.

FROM ANNIE DILLARD:

Now we are no longer primitive; now the whole world seems not-holy. We have drained the light from the boughs in the sacred grove and snuffed it in the high places and along the banks of sacred streams. We as a people have gone from pantheism to pan-atheism.

The Liberal and the Conservative
Shall Lie Down Together

From whose womb did the ice come forth, and who has given birth to the hoarfrost of heaven? The waters become hard like stone and the face of the deep is frozen.

FROM THE BOOK OF JOB

A FROSTY CLIMB up our small misty mountain this week under a smoke-gray sky spitting snow showed that the cold is slowly getting a grip on the mountain. The ground is frozen solid in most places and thumps like a drum when struck with a walking stick. The small brooks are still trickling but the pools are varnished with ice and sharp frost crystals push up along the banks. The trails, too, are now icy in some places.

Near the summit I thought I heard the sound of children's happy voices coming through the woods to the North and wondered what youngsters could be doing on the chilly heights so early. At the peak I scanned the dark woods to see who might be chattering so gaily. To my surprise and delight, it was a flock of ravens surfing the North wind above the tree-tops, diving, darting, rolling, playing tag, and all the while gurgling and cooing at each other in wild musical abandon. It's been a long time since I've seen such a rousing raven show on Awanadjo, and I came down over the conservation land feeling amply rewarded for my climbing efforts.

The words "conservation" and "conservative" spring from the same Latin root, meaning to preserve, save, protect, or keep. To be conservative is to seek to preserve what is valuable. This is the original meaning, and an ancient and honorable quality in any human, as none would deny. I can think of few who would not claim to be conservative in this way, and this is the heart of the conflict between liberalism and conservatism today. It is misleading to call someone 'a conservative' or 'a liberal' because all of us have a little of both in our make-up, and both qualities have long been deemed admirable. To use myself as an example, I love to display our American flag, I have been a gun-owner all my adult life, and I read the Bible. On the other hand, I don't think anyone should be forced to honor the flag, I support background checks, and I don't believe everything the Bible says. So what am I?

To use liberal and conservative as insulting, derisive name tags to be hung on those with whom we differ on a few points is not only wrong grammatically, it is wrong ethically and politically. It abuses the truths and virtues of both, and it murders dialogue. This 'my-way-or-the-highway' mantra is dragging our nation down.

So, let your inner conservative out. Save and protect what is good. Don't be too quick to discard the wisdom of the past. Be thrifty and cautious about what is valuable. Be faithful to your family, friends and country. President Eisenhower, who has been getting quite a makeover recently, reportedly said, "Be conservative when it comes to money, and liberal when it comes to people." This is good advice, showing that a good person can be both. Maybe that's why we liked Ike. Let's take it to heart, and move our country and all our people ahead together.

FROM AMBROSE BIERCE:
A conservative:
One who is enamored of existing evils, as distinguished from a liberal who wishes to replace them with others.

To Hell with Hell

"JOHN ANSWERED ALL OF THEM by saying, 'I baptize you with water; but one who is more powerful than I is coming; I am not worthy to untie the thong of his sandals. He will baptize you with the Holy Spirit and with fire.' Now when all the people were baptized, and when Jesus also had been baptized and was praying, the heaven was opened, and the Holy Spirit descended upon him in bodily form like a dove. And a voice came from heaven, 'You are my Son, the Beloved; with you I am well pleased.'"

This is the Luke account of the baptism of Jesus by John in the Jordan River. When we hear this we might say, "O that is nice, being baptized by water and by the Holy Spirit; that sounds good. Sounds soothing like the 23rd psalm. But what is this about being baptized by fire? That doesn't sound so good." When we hear about baptism by fire we may begin to think of the torments of the early martyrs or the diabolical cruelties of the Inquisition or the unquenchable flames of Hell. Is John trying to frighten people here? Trying to frighten people into certain beliefs has a long history, but it must ultimately fail.

Listen to Hosea Ballou [1771-1852] a radical reformer who believed that every soul will eventually be redeemed:

It is well known, and will be acknowledged by every candid person, that the human heart is capable of becoming soft, or hard; kind, or unkind; merciful or unmerciful, by education and habit. On this principle we contend, that the infernal torments [of Hell] ...have tended so to harden the hearts of the professors of this religion, that they have exercised, toward their fellow creatures, a spirit of enmity, which but too well corresponds with the relentless cruelty of their doctrine, and the wrath which they have imagined to exist in our heavenly Father. By having such an example constantly before their eyes, they have become so transformed into its image …that the cruelty of their doctrine had overcome the native kindness and compassion of the human heart.

This is the tragedy of cruel, angry dogma, and it still haunts our dreams. But the God we seek is not looking for reasons to throw us into an eternal, infernal torture chamber. The God we seek will kindly and lovingly provide us with everything we need and more than we could ever need. Thomas Paine, in *The Age of Reason*, declares, "Do we not see a fair creation prepared to receive us the instant we are born—a world furnished to our hands, that cost us nothing? Is it we that light up the sun, that pour down the rain, and fill the earth with abundance?"

Why would a Creator who provides everything needful for life in great beauty, who tenderly takes our bodies when we die and turns them into earth to nourish other lives all around, a God who wastes nothing and brings everything back to life, why would such a Creator turn around and waste and cruelly destroy a human soul?

No, Hell is a product of human fear and judgment, a bludgeon of angry preachers and a tool of frustrated prophets. And to hell with Hell.

HENRY DAVID THOREAU:
Live in the present, launch yourself on every wave, find your eternity in each moment. Fools stand on their island of opportunities and look toward another land. There is no other land; there is no other life than this.

Talking to God

I HAVE MENTIONED that I treasure a copy of the devotional book that belonged to my father which is called *The Practice of the Presence of God* by Brother Lawrence. Brother Lawrence's 'spiritual practice' is simply a constant intimate conversation with God no matter where Lawrence happens to find himself, whether at prayers, washing pots and pans, mopping, or working in the monastery garden. He finds "that in order to form a habit of conversing with God continually, and referring all we do to Him, we must first apply to Him with some diligence; but that after a little care we should find his love [will] inwardly excite us to it."

This constant conversation and referring all we do to God brings God closer to us and us closer to God. And if God is present in our everyday conversation and work, then gradually God will not be so far away ever. After a time, the conversation is not so critical because the presence becomes more or less constant and familiar. Some of the deepest conversations are silent. Maybe a little like being married for a long time.

I also like the medieval Irish theologian John Scotus Erigena's saying, "Whatever is, is God." This means that other people and creatures, tools, toys, things, frustration, impatience, anger are all aspects of the divine. We are never not with God. God is not over there and we over here. God is the great reality of which everything else is a part. God is here.

If we are practicing the presence of God, then we are inviting God be present to set our priorities and put our lives in order. We're letting God draw up our 'to do' list for today, not other people and creatures, tools, toys, things, frustration, impatience, anger, etc. This way, all the things we have to do everyday need not be distractions from God; they can be attractions to God, or encounters with God, or even adventures with God. I know this to be true.

This sort of spirituality takes practice until it becomes habit. Leaning on the everlasting arms takes two. The arms are there, but we have to be willing to do the leaning. The presence is there for us, if we are willing to be present too. It is much more difficult if God is a faraway angry judge, sitting on high jotting down our infractions in the Book of Life and waiting to punish us. It is much easier if God is love divine, a compassionate presence who understands our failures and our suffering and will stay with us always and never reject us if we will keep the conversation open.

But we need to do our part, hold up our end of the conversation, and listen, too. Have you ever sat down for a talk with someone and found that they keep trying to direct the conversation the way they want it to go? Not listening to you, not hearing, not understanding what you have to say? It gets tiring to the point that you may stop listening. Maybe we sound that way to God, sometimes. That is the lesson here. If we want someone to hear us, we need to be listening, too. We need to be available for God's purposes as much as we expect God to be available for our purposes.

Finally, we're back to baptism by fire. Baptism by fire does not mean punishment or eternal damnation to Hell by an angry God. We can let that horror go once and for all. We all will have to walk through the fire at times: the death of a loved one, loneliness, depression, disease, failure, fear, remorse, trouble and trial. There is no life on earth without the fire walk. But we need not go it alone. Is there some one you would want to go through the fire with you? Then, you will be ready to go through the fire with that one. And together, you will. God does not want us to go through any fire alone. God wants to go through every fire with us. That is the gospel promise.

FROM THE BOOK OF ISAIAH:
Thus says the Lord...
Do not fear, for I have redeemed you;
I have called you by name, you are mine.

When you pass through the waters, I will be with you;
and through the rivers, they shall not drown you;
when you walk through fire you shall not be burned,
and the flame shall not consume you.
Do not fear, for I have redeemed you.

Still Here

YEARS AGO, halfway out the Leighton Point Road in West Pembroke, there was a dilapidated farmhouse which belonged to Martha Sprague, if I remember right. The roof sagged, the chimneys leaned, the clapboards showed no signs of paint, and lilacs and alders grew tall and untamed in the front yard. But your eye was invariably drawn up to the high dormer windows filled with bright green and red geraniums pressed eagerly against the glass. I admired those geraniums and the old woman who lovingly and tenaciously tended them in that bleak house. They said, "I'm still here. I can still love. I haven't given up." The house has fallen down long since, and I've often wondered whether her geraniums died in the wreckage or were saved to brighten someone else's windows in Winter. There was a similar old farmhouse and barn on Route 1A between Holden and Brewer with geraniums in the windows. Maybe they're still there. I hope so.

Abraham Lincoln observed, "The Lord must love common people; since He made so many of them." Geraniums are like that: tough, hardy, and low-maintenance. They can take sun or frost or heavy cutting and come back stronger and brighter than ever.

In honor of that unquenchable spirit, we keep our dozen or so aged geraniums in the windows throughout the Winter. We talk to them, deadhead them, feed and water them just like members of the family. They always bend toward the sun. Each morning we see our flourishing geraniums first, before we look farther out to the bare trees and the pale expanses of frozen ground all around us. This gives us, and anyone who looks in our windows, a feast of color and life and a taste of faith and hope to brighten the bleak days of January.

Faith needs to be tended, too. You don't get faith once and for all with no effort. It needs regular care. Faith and belief are not the same. Belief is like an artificial flower that doesn't change or grow and needs no tending. Faith is like a geranium. It is a living thing that needs good food, fresh water, pure light and fresh air. Looking out over the bleak January landscape of America—a landscape marked by fear, factions, and faltering faith—I say give us geraniums, in the windows of the school house and the town house, the food pantry and the thrift shop. Give us geraniums in the windows of the State House, the Blaine House, the White House, the House of JP Morgan, both Houses of Congress, and every house of correction. Give us geraniums to say, "We're still here. We can still love. We haven't given up." Geraniums in Winter windows will help the few who are on the inside looking out, and they will help the many who are on the outside looking in, because without faith, hope and love, even the greatest nation or people will too soon wither and die.

TERRY TEMPEST WILLIAMS:
Faith is the centerpiece of a connected life. It allows us to live by the grace of invisible strands. It is a belief in a wisdom superior to our own. Faith becomes a teacher in the absence of fact.

Eat Your Boots

I dreamed a dream and I thought it true
Concerning Franklin and his gallant crew
Through cruel hardships they vainly strove
Their ships on mountains of ice they drove
The lonely Eskimo with his skin canoe
Was the only one who made it through.

LADY FRANKLIN'S LAMENT 1852

SURVIVAL IN THE WILD NORTH in Winter can be risky as the fate of
the lost Franklin expedition shows. Sir John Franklin and 128 crew
left England in Summer 1845 to find the Northwest Passage and
over the next several years all were lost in the barren, unforgiving
Arctic. Twenty search expeditions over many decades found bones
and artifacts and Inuit legends indicating that the men died from
cold, starvation, lead poisoning, scurvy, inadequate clothing, and
just plain not buttoning up.

Ernest Thompson Seton [1860-1946], woodcrafter and early
survivalist, says about surviving in the cold North: "For a man who
is lost, the three great dangers, in order of importance, are Fear,
Cold, and Hunger. He may endure extreme hunger for a week, and
extreme cold for a day, but extreme fear may undo him in an hour.
There is no way of guarding against this greatest danger excepting
by assuring him that he is fortified against the other two." Seton
goes on to list foods to be found in a Northern Winter, including
snowshoe hare, mice, ants, wood grubs, and boot leather. On eating
ones boots, he quotes Mark Twain on such an occasion saying "The
holes tasted the best." Seton also suggests any fungus growing on
rotten wood and several kinds of lichens as foods. The most available
lichens are Iceland moss *cetraria icelandica*, a large flattened species
that looks a bit like seaweed; reindeer moss *cladonia rangiferina*, the
fine gray-green variety that grows on open ledges; and rock tripe

umbilicaria arctica which grows on the side of boulders and upright ledges. These, like your boots, are best boiled first.

It seems that the Franklin expedition was killed by two things: too little preparation and too much grandiosity. Franklin insisted that his officers wear standard issue British uniforms, silk braid, brass buttons and all. These were clearly not adequate for the conditions. Their ships were elegant enough, but couldn't withstand the pressures of being frozen into sea ice for so long. Searchers found monogrammed silverware and china plates and poorly made tin cans soldered with lead next to frozen corpses, or so the story goes. The Franklin expedition has become a metaphor for the pride of Empire coming before its fall; trying to prove its superiority over others, trying to impose its will on the vast uninterested powers of Nature, trying to bend the laws of earth and sky and history to its own conceits, trying and failing, and then blaming it on the weather, or the food, or the natives.

FROM ANNIE DILLARD:
Polar explorers... went, I say, partly in search of the sublime, and they found it the only way it can be found, here or there—around the edges, tucked into the corners of the days... [D]espite the purity of their conceptions, they man-hauled their humanity to the Poles.

AND FROM WILLIAM PENN:
Humility and knowledge in poor clothes excel pride and ignorance in costly attire.

The Cloud of Unknowing

TRADITION SAYS JESUS spent forty days and nights in the wilderness being tested and tempted. If he was anything like us, which he was, then this was surely not the beginning of his testing and temptation, and not the end of it either. I would guess that for most of us only four temptations in forty days would be a relief. I don't know about you, but I am more likely to have forty temptations in four days. But that will be the extent of my confessions for now.

Uncounted thousands of words have been uttered about this episode in the life of Jesus, but if I were asked to gather all the temptations of Jesus in the wilderness under one heading, I might say that he was being tempted to put the letter of the law above the spirit of the law or to put literalism above love. He was being tempted to put head above heart.

Jerry DeWitt reached a crisis in his life at the age of 41. He was a dedicated evangelical preacher serving smaller churches in Louisiana. One night he got a phone call from a friend asking him to pray for her brother who was seriously injured in a motorcycle accident and might not live. DeWitt tried to comfort her, but, try as he might, he could not bring himself to pray for her injured brother. DeWitt hung up the phone and wept because he had lost his faith in a bearded white man in the sky who answers your prayers with a "Yes" if you just believe in Him. Within a few days he had found the Clergy Project, an online support group for religious leaders who have lost the faith they once held and no longer hold supernatural beliefs. DeWitt has become very active in another organization called "Recovering from Religion" whose purpose is to help people extricate themselves from evangelical Christianity as he has done himself.

Here's another one: Nate Phelps is the son of Fred Phelps,

leader of the Westboro Baptist Church which picketed funerals and gay pride events with signs saying "God Hates Fags." Nate Phelps is a big, burly bear of a man who delivers fierce and fiery rebuttals of his father's theology. Phelps has become a bit of a guru at atheist and gay pride events. Jerry DeWitt and Nate Phelps have joined the growing reaction to dogmatic religion whether Catholic or Protestant, Jewish or Muslim.

How can people who were once firm in their beliefs do an abrupt about-face like this and become just the opposite of what they were? How can conviction so suddenly become contradiction? I am going to come back to these questions in a minute, but to get there, I want to first walk us through the Cloud of Unknowing.

You may remember the story of the transfiguration when Jesus and the disciples climbed Mt Tabor together. At the top, they were suddenly covered by a cloud and heard the voice of the Lord speaking to them out of the cloud. This episode echoes the time when Moses went up into a cloud covering the top of Mt Sinai where Yahweh spoke to Moses out of the cloud giving him the law. In the soft density of the cloud the voice is heard but the deity is not seen. The presence of God is obscured, unseen by the human eye.

The eye was traditionally considered to be the most reliable of the senses, because after all, hearing is only hearing, but seeing is believing. So it was that through the ages, God could sometimes be heard, but never seen, always hidden in clouds.

In the mid-14th century an anonymous English Christian composed a work on contemplative prayer called the Cloud of Unknowing which has become a devotional classic. It arose out of a Christian neo-Platonist tradition. In some seventy-six chapters written in dense and intricate Middle English the author—perhaps a monk or a nun—stresses that God cannot be known by the human mind, but only by the heart. The Cloud of Unknowing has opened the hearts of many seekers through the years including the medieval mystics Nicolas of Cusa and John of the Cross and continuing down to Evelyn Underhill and Teilhard de Chardin in the mid-20th century and on to the centering prayer movement of Thomas Keating and Cynthia Bourgeault right up to the present day.

Here is a little bit of it:

For He can well be loved, but He cannot be thought. By love He can be grasped and held, but by thought neither grasped nor held. And therefore, though it may be good at times to think specifically about the kindness and excellence of God, and though this may be a light and a part of contemplation, all the same in the work of contemplation itself, it must be cast down and covered with a cloud of forgetting. And you must step above it stoutly but deftly with a devout and delightful stirring of love, and struggle to pierce that darkness above you; and beat on that thick cloud of unknowing with a sharp dart of longing love, and do not give up, whatever happens.

What was Jesus doing for forty days and nights in the wilderness? Was he memorizing the laws in the book of Leviticus? Was he studying theology? Was he writing an ordination paper or a dissertation? Was he reviewing his catechism, polishing his rhetoric? I don't think so. I think he was pushing against that thick cloud of unknowing with his longing love. And he was getting through. He was contemplating, he was meditating, he was listening, he was confronting his own weaknesses and preparing for a life of natural love in action regardless of what the consequences might be for him.

Love is not a supernatural concept, it is a natural activity. Love in action is raising a family and taking care of each other.

Love in action is feeding the hungry and clothing the naked regardless of whether they have filled out all the forms correctly to prove their eligibility.

Love in action puts the well-being of real life human beings and all creatures above the pronouncements of dead theologians, or living theologians, or politicians, or social service bureaucrats.

Love in action puts compassion for all creatures first: "Most good, least harm," as Zoe Weil puts it.

Love in action is plowing out someone else's driveway, starting a food drive, supporting a heating fund, taking a covered dish to someone.

Love in action is one person telling a bully to stop and it is a billion rising to stop violence against women anywhere in the world.

It seems to me that Jerry DeWitt and Nate Phelps and so many others like them lost their faith because their supernatural belief, their dogma and doctrine, could no longer support their faith. Belief is useless, maybe even dangerous, unless it leads to love in action. Even if you believe in the flying spaghetti monster but still love your neighbor as yourself, you are a better Christian than if you believe every word of the King James Bible and the Westminster catechism and despise your neighbor.

It's not so much a question of belief on the one hand or unbelief on the other hand. It's more like belief and unbelief on the one hand or love and wonder on the other hand. Belief and unbelief are not opposites, they are just different degrees of the same thing, they are two sides of the same coin, they are functions of the head, not of the heart, and ultimately they cannot penetrate the cloud of unknowing. But love and wonder are functions of the heart, and they can see through the clouds to God.

For God can well be loved, but God cannot be thought. By thought God cannot be grasped or held, but by love God can be both grasped and held.

Darkness at Noon

Nothing in this world is really precious until we know that it will soon be gone. The lily, the starry daffodil, the regal iris... are the lovelier for their imminent vanishing. The snow crystal has but touched the earth ere it begins to die.

FROM AMERICAN NATURALIST DONALD CULROSS PEATTIE 1898-1964

A RARE RENDEZVOUS between one storm blasting eastward off the Great Lakes and another barreling up the Atlantic Coast brought us a blizzard of mythic proportions just before the New *Snow* Moon. It was the kind of snow storm that memories are made of. The wind was blowing a gale for the better part of two days sending the snow sideways and causing white-out conditions for hours on end. Some of the fluffy white that finally settled in the back yard could have blown there from Prince Edward Island for all we know. If we could have heard the wind as it moaned in all the chimneys in the village at once it would have sounded like God's own bag-pipes. On the windward side of our old house there was snow on the inside window sills blown in around the closed windows. Along with the roaring winds the air was bitter cold causing deadly wind chills, and yet at the height of the storm a lonely nuthatch worked the downwind side of the big pear tree outside our kitchen window and a few hardy chickadees flew to the feeders and then blew back into the cover of nearby shrubs. The plowmen came by several times to move some snow trying to stay ahead of the storm. Even at 10:00 in the morning it was so dark they were running all their lights. The energy of the storm was so exhilarating that your commentator felt like an excited kid wanting to go out and play.

So I bundled up and shoveled the walks again and again, while the cut I made through the growing drifts filled right up again behind me as I went along. It was a fruitless task, but so much better than sitting indoors waiting for the storm to end while the joints seized up and the arteries hardened. When we retired for the second night of the storm the trees were still thrashing back and forth in the dark, the chimneys were howling and the old windows rattling like some unknown nocturnal creature trying to get in out of the cold. When the storm finally broke on the third day more marvels were revealed. There were drifts of four or more feet in some spots and other spots where the ground was blown bare. The trees were utterly bare of snow thanks to the fierce cleansing of the wind. The sky turned blue and the wind died, but not the plow-men. They finished up their work quite nicely and retired home for a good half day and full night of rest.

You know, with all the talk these days of climate change and storms of the century, we get pretty worked up about the weather. But your commentator has seen three score and fifteen northern winters and this storm left him with a feeling not of anxiety or worry or fear but of satisfaction and gratitude: satisfaction at having enjoyed another old-fashioned, full-fledged, gold-plated, star-spangled, rip-roaring nor'easter with all the trimmings, and gratitude that we still know how to keep the roads plowed and the walks shoveled and the heat and lights on and still make it to church or to grandmother's house the morning after. It was an historic storm, the storm of the century. And we're ready for another.

FROM JOHN BANISTER TABB:
Are ye the ghosts of fallen leaves, O flakes of snow, For which, through naked trees, the winds a-mourning go?"

Slow Down

The days of our years are threescore years and ten, and if by reason of strength they be fourscore years, yet is their strength labour and sorrow; for it is soon cut off and we fly away.

FROM PSALM 90

ONE OF THE MANY THINGS to love about Winter is having enough time. We have two rope-seated, spindle-legged, straight-back chairs—one red, one blue—on either side of the 1905 Glenwood stove in the kitchen. There's nothing like an hour, or even two, spent there. You know how they say the older you get the faster time goes? Maybe age has nothing to do with it. Time is a function of motion: if there were no motion there would be no time. Like so much around us, the velocity of our lives increases year by year, so time seems to accelerate, too. I used to have a 1960 Dodge D-100 panel truck that had a cruising speed of about 45. The windshield wipers had only one speed, so if you went over 45, the wipers couldn't stay ahead of the rain. That was only about 50 years ago. Fifty years before that the model T had a top speed of about the same. Today these couldn't legally be driven on Interstate highways; they'd be a slow hazard. The recent collision of 70 or more vehicles that turned several miles of I-95 into a vast junk yard happened because people were going too fast for conditions.

The great medieval cathedrals of Europe each took a century or more in construction, while the world's tallest man-made structure, the Dubai Tower, took only five years to build. Olympic speed-skating is shown on prime-time while curling is shown in the wee hours. We have clocks on our wrists, our cell phones, our computers and our appliances, clocks in every room. And yet we never seem to have enough time; we're always in a hurry. Meanwhile, stress is killing us. Doctors are busy treating stress-related diseases of the body. Therapists are busy treating stress-related diseases of the mind and soul. To relax, we rush off to the airport to fly at 400 miles per hour to hectic vacation spots, and then we rush back exhausted. We have no time for timelessness.

Meanwhile, the seasons still change at the same slow pace they have always kept. The sun still rises and sets no faster than ever. The planets ponderously move as they always did. And the length of our lives is still three-score and ten or four-score years as it was when the Psalms were set down three thousand years ago. So what's the big hurry?

That's why it's so blissful to lose all track of time in simply daydreaming or reading or just sitting by the stove thinking on a blustery night. I like to take my own sweet time, and won't easily let someone else take it from me. That's why you may see me driving through town at five miles under the speed limit instead of ten over. Maybe I can add a couple of minutes to the precious life of that impatient driver on my tail.

We evolved at walking speed—about four miles an hour. Do you want to live longer? Slow down. Do you want your children to live longer? Slow them down. Let them get bored now and then. Let them see you do nothing for a while. Walk and talk. Sit and think. Squeeze all the juice out of every moment. Make some space in your schedule for eternity. You may live longer or you may not, but guaranteed, you'll live better.

FROM EUDORA WELTY:
Events in our lives happen in a sequence in time, but in their significance to ourselves, they find their own order in the continuous thread of revelation.

FROM ANNIE DILLARD:
How we spend our days is, of course, how we spend our lives.

I'll Never Forget What's-His-Name

Something remains for us to do or dare;
even the oldest tree some fruit may bear…
For age is opportunity no less
than youth itself, though in another dress;
And as the evening twilight fades away,
the sky is filled with stars, invisible by day.

HENRY WADSWORTH LONGFELLOW

AGING IS A NATURAL EVENT, but there's so much they just don't tell you ahead of time. In a youth-obsessed culture, passing 50 or 60 or [gasp!] 70 is a little like being cast out into the wilderness without a map. Yet, there are many marvels and mysteries to be revealed to open eyes and minds in those farther fields. First, some cautions: Remember the 20/40 rule. Around 40 and beyond we tend to think of ourselves as roughly 20 years younger than we really are. It's good to keep in mind that we're not. Try not to impress people by doing things that you haven't done since you were 20. This will prevent a lot of embarrassment. There is no fool like an old fool. Some of the most famous last words are: "Hey guys, watch this!" Next, that whooshing sound in your ears is probably *tinnitus* caused by gradual hearing loss. There's no cure, but you can make it worse by taking aspirin. You may want to remove your bifocals when going down stairs, gangways, or mountains. Don't try too hard to remember a name; it's more likely to come if you don't think about it, though by then it's often too late. Be alert to those new bumps that appear on your body and show them to your doctor. Get used to hair growing where it never did and not growing where it always has. Remind yourself that gray hair is a mark of distinction. Try a home blood pressure monitor; it can help you keep your BP down. Worry, regret and anger are corrosive of the spirit. Prepare for the worst, hope for the best; then don't worry.

Apologize if you've done someone wrong; then let it go. What others do to you is their karma; what you do to them is yours. Jealousy and envy are poison to the spirit. Don't compare yourself to others; compare yourself to your former self.

Now, some wonders that may be beheld in those vast and varied lands past 40: One finds that love mixed with a good measure of forgiveness is the universal solvent, and remedy—miraculously smoothing over rough spots, dissolving problems, and healing wounds. You may find that you are less full of yourself, and more full of life itself. In the first part of life you discover how unlike your ancestors you are. In the second part you may discover how much you are like them; your joys and sorrows and humor are less personal and more universal; you discover that we really are all in this equally together. This can be vastly comforting, revealing a beautiful new landscape where you are free to live the rest of your life in the company of every living creature, if you so desire. The longer you live, the more you can grow.

And at the very last, naturally, there is the greatest revelation of all. As the body weakens and fails, the soul gets wiser and stronger from weathering storms and squalls, until it takes its final flight on strong, bright wings.

SIDDHARTHA GAUTAMA, THE BUDDHA:
The secret of health for both mind and body is not to mourn for the past, not to worry about the future, but to live the present moment wisely and earnestly.

RALPH WALDO EMERSON:
As we grow old, the beauty steals inward.

It's Dying Time Again

WINTER IS A DYING TIME, just look at the two or more pages of death notices in the paper each day. The other day I found a gray squirrel lying still in the middle of the road as though asleep, not a mark on it. But it was not sleeping. I placed it in the pucker-brush beside the road where Nature's undertakers will bring it back to life in the fullness of time, and I pondered where it had gone. Other seasons are times of dying too, but not like Winter, for now the land itself seems cold and dead, locked in ice under gray clouds, as though earth and sky were grieving together. The wind in the chimney moans like a dirge, and even by the fire we shiver. Death is something we'd rather ignore. Biologist Bernd Heinrich is quoted in the New York Times, "Human death is becoming more and more divorced from nature. We pump our dead with polluting chemicals like formaldehyde, put them into airtight boxes and then plant them in precious real estate that could be used for agriculture. We think we're denying death that way." Some believe the purpose of religion is to give us eternal life, and offer magic formulas from the Bible to make it happen. Much of medical science seems to want the same thing. We're told that the greatest medical costs come in the last year of life, striving fruitlessly to avoid the unavoidable, raging against the dying of the light.

But death always comes with a purpose. Everything, everyone dies so that others can live. We will all make the ultimate sacrifice eventually, though when the body is ravaged by injury, pain or disease, letting it go can be less a sacrifice than an exquisite pleasure and a boundless relief unmatched by just about anything else in life. In the end, rich or poor, selfish or unselfish, kind or unkind, willing or unwilling, we all give up our lives for others whether we want to or not. We might as well make it a gift freely given from the heart.

FROM WALT WHITMAN 1819-1892:
Come lovely and soothing death/ Undulate round the world, serenely arriving, arriving/ In the day, in the night, to all, to each/ Sooner or later, delicate death... Dark Mother, always gliding near, with soft feet/ Have none chanted for thee a chant of fullest welcome? Then I chant it for thee.

AND FROM DR MARTIN LUTHER KING JR.:
Like anybody, I would like to live a long life; longevity has its place. But I'm not concerned about that now, I just want to do God's will.

View from the Heights

AWANADJO OR BLUE HILL MOUNTAIN, as the locals call her, is not really a mountain in the strict topographical sense, being just under one thousand feet in altitude. But, she is *our* mountain. She is not Everest, or Denali, or Fuji, or Katahdin. But, she is *our* Everest, Denali, Fuji, or Katahdin. And she is our Holy Mountain. From the summit we look down on the world as it is "*sub specie aeternitatis*"—under the gaze of the eternal. We look down at the world as the Creator does. And what do we see? We see forests and hills to the West and North. We see coastline, islands and open sea to the East and South. Beyond the islands, the sea falls off over the edge of the earth, appearing endless. Likewise, the forests and hills disappear over the far horizon, though on a very clear day, Katahdin may appear as a faint shadow far off to the Northwest. We see the enormity and beauty of the works of Nature and the insignificance of the works of man.

All the rushing about from store to bank to post office to hospital to school, all the coming and going, the getting and spending, the hammering and honking are absolutely invisible and inaudible from the mountain. The labors of men and machines for two centuries have changed the look of the town very little. It is still just a rough and slightly raw patch surrounded by a vast living, growing wildness. Looking down on the village we can barely make out the steeples of three churches which from the height appear almost identical, even though those who gather within them are convinced that their differences are great enough that very few would consider attending all three.

If we were to be taken up onto the highest mountain in the world, the human suffering and strife, the wars and the warriors, the frantic markets and the frenzied martyrs, the masters of war and the masters of greed, would disappear, engulfed in the vast roundness of the Earth, the Body of God, living, breathing, growing, dying and living again ever so slowly and patiently. It is one Earth, one Body, when viewed from the height. This great body has one natural hope and desire, that is, life. It has one indigenous and universal religion, that is, to live and die so that others may live and die. It has one true and absolutely practical creed, expressed in all the world's faiths, that is, to do to others what you would have them do to you. Looking out from the summit, we see how little we really need, yet how much we demand from this great body. The most disquieting thing we see is how great the Earth is, and how small we are. This is what our eyes see.

What our hearts see is this: If we do not follow the creed of the Earth; if we do not pass the simple test which She gives to all creatures; if we do not understand the Tough Love that She practices, then the hair and bone of our kind will be carefully gathered up by her and turned into soil and rock for the quiet and gentle advancement of Her holy purposes.

There are those who will call this view from the heights romantic and sentimental. They would do very well to get out of their climate-controlled offices with their flat angles and surfaces, out of their cars and black SUVs, away from their lying spin doctors, sycophantic yes-men, and brutish body-guards; far away from their big bucks, their big bombers and big bombs; out to where they are all equally creatures; out to where they can see Mother Nature's sharp, gaunt, huge and hungry teeth.

They would do very well to struggle alone up a mountain in Maine in late March.

FROM WALT WHITMAN 1819-1892:
There can be no theory of any account unless it corroborate the theory of the earth,/No politics, song, religion, behavior, or what not, is of account, unless it compare with the amplitude of the earth,/Unless it face the exactness, vitality, impartiality, rectitude of the earth.

SPRING

Hope

ALTHOUGH HARDLY NOTICEABLE, the miracle of Spring began this past week, a few days later to be followed by the miracle of Easter. So the question is this: are miracles natural events or un-natural? Or supernatural? Anything can happen when we don't have our minds made up. The trouble is that too many people—believers and unbelievers alike—start each day with their minds made up, even before their beds are made up. This is the prison of belief whose walls are demolished by the miraculous. What is a miracle but something we thought could never happen? What but a natural miracle could bring a chaos of undifferentiated matter and energy together to form an orderly cosmos with galaxies, stars and circling planets, at least one and possibly millions of which harbor the miracle of life? What but a natural miracle could cause simple single-celled organisms to coalesce and evolve into beautiful singing birds and talking, thinking primates who discover the marvels of evolution, e-mail, reggae and sushi? What but a miracle could end the bloodshed in Northern Ireland or South Africa? There's a model for the whole weary world.

It is your commentator's opinion that miracles are neither supernatural nor un-natural but profoundly natural events, if we have eyes to see. The burden of proof should fall on the nay-sayers. You say there is no such thing as a miracle? Then prove it. Ptolemy proved that the sun orbits the earth, and Copernicus proved that it does not. It's been proven that light is both a wave and a particle. Only open eyes, open minds, and open hearts can see the miraculous. If you find yourself slipping over into anger, fear or bitterness, ask yourself this: What would it cost me to give the benefit of the doubt to the possibility of God and miracles and life overcoming death? How hard could that be? We're not talking about donating a kidney here. Why not make wonder my fall-back position rather than cynicism? Why not make joy and hope my default mode rather than sorrow and despair? Ask yourself what works better, everyday, in town and on the ground. Does my day go better when I go out with hope in my heart, or with fear? Am I more happy, creative and productive when I see the universe as a cruel and heartless dead machine, or when I see it as a miraculous and soulful living being? Get practical. Try it for a couple of days and see. It's free.

Snow Melt

As a hart longs for flowing streams, so longs my soul for thee...
Deep calls to deep at the thunder of thy cataracts; all thy waves
and thy billows have gone over me. As a hart longs for flowing
streams, so longs my soul for thee, O living God.

BOOK OF PSALMS

APRIL SHOWERS HAVE MELTED the snow and ice with gratifying speed and now, after months of deathly torpor, life is rapidly returning here. The clogged arteries of the land are miraculously cleared. The earthy breath comes fresh again. The body warms and the heart of the earth beats stronger. The ice is gone from the streams and mostly gone from the harbor where the mill brook turns the waters the color of *cafe au lait* with runoff from upstream; and the brook's roar can be heard all through the village. The stump of the old sugar maple cut down during the Winter is now welling up with fresh sap from the roots. Along Maine's rivers and streams, paddlers shake off the chill and limber up on the muddy banks in readiness for the traditional canoe races that add some competitive spirit to the month of April while the playing fields are still too wet for playing, and the working fields too wet for working. Life and movement are once more restored and we watch the long-awaited miracle of resurrection happening right before eyes. We mortals return to life too: some sooner, some later. In the old days, we are told, there were Spring tonics concocted to drive Winter's sluggishness away. Grandma would soak some nails in a bucket of water until it turned orange and then everyone would drink. Dandelion leaves were steeped into tea. Sour rhubarb stems were chewed [as long as you could stand it] to freshen the blood and motivate you to get the Spring chores done before the black-flies returned.

The snowy owls are gone, but look up for turkey vultures soaring with slightly upturned wings on gentle thermals rising above the South face of Awanadjo. Look down for rumpling woolly bear caterpillars out for a stroll. And look ahead for the first butterfly of spring, the Mourning Cloak, which is the only butterfly in Maine that winters over as an adult. And we think WE had a rough Winter! How in heaven do they survive?

Town meeting is done again for another year. It is always time well-spent, if for nothing else than to see the cast of characters sitting in their usual seats and playing out their usual roles: the moderator banging his gavel, the budget committee firmly urging austerity, the school committee earnestly reminding us of the importance of education, the fire chief mentioning how that old pumper is wearing out, the newcomer from Massachusetts telling us how they do it there, the bake sales, the turkey dinner by the seventh grade—all of it. It is so real, so fine, and so precious. Let us never forget.

Left behind by the melting snow is a whole Winter's worth of litter and trash strewn along the roadside. Consider for a moment the carelessness of the attitude that I can throw away anything I don't want and someone else will clean it up. That attitude is not just about beer cans and used diapers, either. It is also about acres of spent nuclear fuel rods, rivers of spilled crude, lakes of fracking by-products, and mountains of toxic mine tailings. The earth can give us all we need to be content forever, but it can't give us absolutely everything we might ever possibly crave. All we see around us is a gift from the Creator. It is not a trash dump.

There I go getting preachy again, but then what can you expect from a preacher?

Migrating shore birds are passing through on their way North including yellow-legs, plovers and sandpipers. Funnel-shaped 'fyke' nets are staked open in rivers and streams to capture tiny elvers or 'glass eels' to be shipped live to Asia to be farmed to full size and eagerly eaten.

FROM *ROLL ON, PENOBSCOT,* BY THE AUTHOR:
With Spring's melting snow from Katahdin's steep side, mile after mile of whitewater you ride, from Maine's highest mountain to her lowest tide, you roll on Penobscot, roll on.

From Iceland to Ireland

IT IS BREATH-TAKING, really, how much the world around us has changed since the last full moon. After months of living on Planet Drear, everything is now decked out in lucid glowing green. It is easy to forget, over the course of a long Winter [and every Winter in Maine is a long Winter] just how green everything becomes when Spring sweeps in at last. It's like going from Iceland to Ireland without even leaving home. Where a short time ago every plant had withdrawn into itself for its own survival, now billions upon billions of tiny solar cells burst forth to make food in abundance for all creatures and distribute it profligately in the ancient alchemy of life on Earth. Underground, the vast unseen networks of roots and fungal mycelia are awakened to share food and moisture with each other far and wide. From craggy hilltop to valley swale flowers open their bright blossoms of intricate symmetry to pollination by wind or bug or bird. Perfumes fill the air. Birds of many colors add their songs. All that was bare and barren is now fertile and flushed with life, sharing what it has with every other creature with perfect generosity.

The blueberry barrens are decked in shades of bronze, rust and lime as the tiny leaves emerge and their bell-like flowers call to the bees. On the forest floor Canada Mayflower, Lily-of-the-Valley and Starflower are coming into bloom, along with Bunchberry and Viburnum on the margins of the woods. Apple, pear, and cherry bloom are coming along and the work of making fruit has begun. We noticed a few hayfields already cut this week, with hay lying in windrows waiting for the baler. Gardeners are not wanting for rain, but maybe a little more sun, please

Our small misty mountain again lives up to its name these days as cool damp mornings send wispy veils of mist curling up from the slopes like the ghosts of old growth forests, giving the whole mountain a dream-like appearance and reminding us of the leafy Titans that once held their ground there.

The same organic transformation going on all around us can happen within us, too, if we are willing. Like the trees, we can go from supplication to praise, from stingy to generous, from inward to outward. Like the flowers, we can open ourselves to the life around us and give what we have to give indiscriminately, without concern that those who receive are deserving or undeserving, righteous or unrighteous, conservative or liberal, correct or incorrect. In this season we can go easily from selfish to unselfish, from sinner to saint, in perfect accord with the blooming, bustling, buzzing world around us.

FROM HENRY BESTON 1888 -1968:
Among the many things for which I remain profoundly grateful is the fact that so much of life defies human explanation. The unimaginative and the dull may insist that they have an explanation for everything, and level at every wonder and mystery of life their popgun theories, but God be praised, their wooden guns have not yet dislodged the smallest star.

New Same Old Earth

*The old people came to love the soil and sat or reclined on
the ground with a feeling of being close to a mothering
power. It was good to touch the earth and the old people
liked to… walk with bare feet on the sacred earth. That is
why the old Indian still sits upon the earth to come closer in
kinship to other lives around.*

LUTHER STANDING BEAR 1868-1939

NEW GREEN IS BEGINNING to show on trees and shrubs up and down
the coast. Daffodils are in bloom and dandelions too in sheltered
Southern exposures. How do these plants survive the bitter cold
winters? Their basic survival strategy is to raise the sugar content
of their sap and draw most of it down into the roots underground
when the growing season ends and the cold winds begin to blow.
Just enough is kept in the buds to keep them alive until the sun
begins to warm the ground and the plant knows it's time to pump
the sap back up, we know not how. During the Winter, these tender
buds on trees and shrubs are protected from the cold by tough bud
scales that cover their soft flesh completely, sort of like us when
we bundle up from head to toe to venture out into the snow. In
Spring, the buds throw off their cloaks and unfurl their leaves and
flowers to the mighty Sun, with a silent cheer for the season ahead.
We do the same. On a sunny day we take off our jackets, maybe
even our shirts, and sit in the sunshine with all new hopes, dreams
and plans dancing in our heads, and the old dog lying beside.

We see in the paper special sales on weed-killer for your yard. They
are practically giving it away. Our advice? Don't buy it, don't use
it, don't even touch it. The World Health Organization declared
recently that the most popular weed-killer in the world "probably causes cancer." Why, in the name of all that is good and holy,

would anyone put anything onto the ground that could cause cancer in their children and grandchildren?

Recall how Stephen Hawking, the late great British physicist, told a gathering at the Sydney Opera House that we must colonize outer space because "I don't think we will survive another 1000 years without escaping our fragile planet." With all due respect to one of the greatest physicists of his generation, this sounds a bit too much like a scientist's version of the Rapture of the Elect delusion so widespread among certain Christians, whereby the chosen are spirited off into the sky leaving the rest of us to suffer here below in the mess they have left behind. Prophecy is not science, and the two should not be confused.

Here are a few questions for Dr Hawking: What is to happen to the several billions of human beings who cannot afford a ticket to Mars? Who decides who goes and who stays? How are these far-flung colonies to survive without massive on-going support from Earth at huge cost to those left behind? Why would anyone think we wouldn't do to Mars just what we are doing to Earth? Wouldn't it be better to simply make the Earth happily habitable? It does no good to sow false hopes for the survival of the human race somewhere someday when what we really need is to work together today with the skills, technology and compassion we have here and now to make the fragile, beautiful, blue-green Earth our home for ages and ages to come until the sun stops shining and the stars fall from the sky.

FROM JULIAN OF NORWICH
Be a gardener, dig a ditch, toil and sweat, and turn the earth upside down, and seek the deepness and water the plants in time. Continue this labor and make sweet floods to run and noble and abundant fruits to spring. Take this food and drink and carry it to God as your true worship.

AND FROM RICHARD POWERS:
The massive tree of life, spreading, branching, flowering. That's all it seems to want to do. To keep making guesses. To go on changing, rolling with the punches.

The Worm Turns

Have been hovering today –
Between the cloud of unknowing above
And the cloud of forgetting below
Being in the clouds is pleasant enough – it's the hovering –
No chopper pad/No place to set down –
Except right here – where the dog is asking for another biscuit.

DEBORAH MOSCOWITZ

THIS PAST WEEK your commentator was walking here and there and noticing small, new holes in the soil with tiny mounds next to them: wormholes and worm castings. Now that the frost is out of the ground, the earthworms have begun their eternal work of plowing up the soil for the new season. Charles Darwin's final book was *The Formation of Vegetable Mould through the Action of Worms, with Observations on their Habits* [1881]. He wrote, "It may be doubted that any other animals have played so important a part in the history of the world as these lowly organized creatures... Without the work of this humble creature, who knows nothing of the benefits he confers on mankind, agriculture, as we know it, would be very difficult, if not impossible." Darwin died the following year, and had hoped to be given to the worms in the local churchyard, but instead was buried with pomp in Westminster Abbey. But the worms will not be cheated forever.

Goldfinches are decked out in their new yellow Spring suits for courting, as juncos and song sparrows call from the woods. Tractors bounce along the roads as Spring plowing is underway where the ground is dry enough. Crocuses and Scilla are in bloom in the dooryard and daffodils and lilies show their green spikes above the dark earth.

Recent rains kept the summit of our mountain obscured by mist while water rushed down the slopes. Vernal pools in the woods are still filled with ice, though spring peepers are calling in warmer pools and ponds. Mosses and lichens luxuriate in sun and rain on the rocky slopes; this is their moment in the sun when they get its undivided attention, until they are shaded again when fresh, new leaves come back to the trees.

It has been debated for ages whether or not animals have feelings like ours. To suggest that they do is to commit the unscientific sin of "anthropomorphizing," making other creatures seem too much like us, thus making it harder to abuse them as we do. Recent research has found fascinating ways in which animals understand death and do mourn and grieve. Elephants may gather around the body of a dead herd-mate for days, crows gather to cover the body of one of their own with grass and twigs, apes protect the bodies of their dead and may carry their dead young for many days. This will not be news to millions who know the ways of animals and feel kinship with them. One morning like this almost 50 years ago your commentator had his eyes opened to new and wilder realms by a crow doing a ritual dance of mourning near the body of another. It changed my life forever.

FROM ELLEN DEGENERES
I ask people why they have deer heads on their walls. They always say because it's such a beautiful animal. There you go. I think my mother is attractive, but I have photographs of her.

AND FROM ANATOLE FRANCE:
Until one has loved an animal, a part of one's soul remains unawakened.

Coming to Our Senses

And this, our life, exempt from public haunt, finds tongues in trees,
books in the running brooks, sermons in stones, and good in everything.

FROM WILLIAM SHAKESPEARE

OVER THE CENTURIES as we have left the country and moved into the cities, we have set a wider and wider gulf between ourselves and other creatures. Our food, which once came from surrounding fields and forests, now comes mostly from feed lots and factory farms far away. Our medicines, which once came from plants, now come from factory laboratories. In our minds, the value of animals is to be measured by their usefulness to us, and not their usefulness to the whole planet. Their muscles become our meat, their skins become our clothing, their young are taken to test our poisons, their heart valves are taken to repair our hearts, the left-over parts of their bodies become toxic garbage, and the ancient wisdom of their ways is lost to us. If it had not been for our cats and dogs and nature programming on TV many of us would have lost touch with the realm of plants and animals entirely.

This isolation from Earth is taking its toll on us. Our sense of smell was fashioned to savor the scent of horses, dogs and cattle, goats and grass, fire and flower. So, when we smell only exhaust fumes, pollution and bad perfume, we lose our sense of the rich and heady aromas that surround real living things.

Our ears were made to hear bird songs, animal calls, rush of wind, roll of thunder. So, when we hear only human voices and human noises, we lose our place in the symphony of the cosmos.

Our eyes were made to scan rolling hills, curving mountains, soft colors and silent beasts moving over the ground. When we see only straight lines, flat surfaces, artificial colors, and shiny wheeled vehicles, we lose sight of the shimmering effulgence of Nature's true light.

Our bodies were formed to walk, to run, to climb, to dig and to build in the open air. When we sit in our homes, then sit it our cars, then sit in our schools and offices, we lose the health of our bodies.

Saddest of all, our souls were marvelously crafted to sense the divinity in every star, planet, leaf, cloud and creature. So, when we find divinity only in concert halls, museums and old books, or nowhere at all, we are in danger of losing our souls. Like prisoners wasting away in a dark cell built by our own hands, we become angry, fearful, depressed, alienated, violent—dangerous to ourselves and others.

We are aching to escape into the living, breathing, blooming, buzzing world, to see, hear, smell, taste, and touch the Earth—created, not by us, but by the one Author of Creation. We are dying to join the chorus of birds and beasts whose carols herald the sun each day, songs of praise to the Creator of us all alike.

The Earth calls us back. So, let's go.

FROM HENRY DAVID THOREAU
Every creature is better alive than dead, men and moose and pine trees, and he who understands it aright will rather preserve its life than destroy it.

FROM E.O. WILSON:
If all mankind were to disappear, the world would regenerate back to the rich state of equilibrium that existed ten thousand years ago. If insects were to vanish, the environment would collapse into chaos.

April

The sun was warm, but the wind was chill.
You know how it is with an April day,
When the sun is out and the wind is still,
You're one month on in the middle of May.
But if you so much as dare to speak,
A cloud comes over the sunlit arch,
A wind comes off a frozen peak,
And you're one month back in the middle of March.

FROM ROBERT FROST 1874-1963

IN NEW ENGLAND they like to say that things are better once we get over "March Hill." Well, we are now over March Hill, but in Maine, it has to be said, April often looks a lot like March. So if you have not yet had enough of frosty nights, chilly mornings, gray and brown landscape, and hauling firewood, fear not, there is still more to come. The nice thing about April, though, is that all of those things are on their way out, exiting stage left. And all the joys of Spring and Summer are waiting to make their entrance stage right [if you are facing North, that is.] That is the exquisite beauty of Spring in Maine; it is a long, teasing season, showing you a hint of splendor and then hiding it again; bathing you in warm sun, then chasing it away with a late flurry of snow. April is a month for mindfulness, for paying attention; because the changes come slowly, so slowly, staying longer every day. Now, there is still frost in the ground, but by the end of the month the grass will be green and the first wildflowers will be in bloom: bluets and violets in the meadows and colt's foot in the ditches. Real things take time. Watch and wait, watch and wait patiently. She is shy, Spring. But she surely comes, closer and closer.

We watch the deer all year, but no more than they watch us. Sometimes we'll go outside thinking of something else and feel their eyes upon us from the field above the bay. We'll look up and there they are with their huge eyes on us missing nothing, their elegant ears taking in every sound we make from a hundred yards away, and their delicate noses sensing the smells of wood smoke and coffee we carry on us. These days they are shedding their winter coats and changing their diet from browse to pasture. You can see the difference in their droppings. Now and then they will start jumping and hopping and chasing each other for no reason, just pure exuberance that Winter is over. Now and then we'll do that too.

FROM MAINE SINGER/SONGWRITER DAVID MALLETT
It's greenin' up real good, lookin' mighty fine
Ev'ry little seed coming right on time
Up across the field and up into the woods
It's greenin' up real good

Whose Earth Is It?

*If we approach nature and the environment without... awe and
wonder, ...then our attitude will be one of masters, consumers,
ruthless exploiters unable to set limits on their immediate needs.
By contrast, if we feel intimately united with all that exists,
then sobriety and care will well up spontaneously.*

FROM POPE FRANCIS

WE ARE IN PEAK WILDFLOWER SEASON right about now with many
iconic plants in bloom. Fields and roadsides are filled with buttercups and daisies with some red clover mixed in. This combination
of colors, smells and textures can make artists swoon, botanists
smile, photographers cheer and the rest of us slip into a trance as
the golden days of childhood flash before our eyes.

Up on the blueberry barrens above the Wardwell pasture, a
heavy crop of berries is turning a pale misty blue and beginning to
size up. When we think of Maine we naturally think of blueberries but there are many more kinds all around us. Among Maine's
edible berries are blueberry, blackberry, bearberry, raspberry, huck-
leberry, elderberry, partridge berry, lingonberry, strawberry, and
serviceberry, also called juneberry. All are good in jams and jellies
and most can be eaten out of hand or dried for later and are high
in anti-oxidants. There are also a number of berries that you might
not want to eat but are valuable for other reasons. Bunchberry is
our Northern dogwood. It has pinnately veined leaves and a four
bract flower like the dogwood tree, but only one flower per plant
growing very close to the ground. The berries grow in a cluster
of bright red in late summer and are not poisonous, but have very
little taste to them. Deer are fond of them. Bayberry is known
throughout New England for its enchanting spicy fragrance and
waxy berries that our forebears used to make aromatic candles.

Saving the worst for last, we have barberry. This thorny plant has white pendant flowers and red tear-drop berries and comes in several varieties with different colors of foliage. Here's why barberry is the bad guy: It is invasive; its berries are poisonous; and it is associated with high incidence of Lyme disease as it provides ideal tick habitat. Do not buy it, do not plant it. If you find it on your property, we suggest you take it out.

Pope Francis's pronouncement on threats to Creation from climate change, *Laudato Si'*, is valuable not just because it was uttered by the leader of a billion or more Catholics all over the world, but because it succinctly brings together in one document the whole "cry of the earth" and imbues it with spiritual power. He condemns the throwaway culture of the developed countries and calls us to "discover God in all things." Read it on-line. You may be glad you did.

POPE FRANCIS:
*We seem to think that we can substitute an irreplaceable and
irretrievable beauty with something we have created ourselves.*

ST FRANCIS:
*Be praised, My Lord, for our sister Mother Earth who feeds us and
governs us and brings forth divers fruits, colorful flowers, and all herbs.*

Nature Heals

A SUPREMELY DETACHED Eastern philosopher once said, "If I could save the whole world by lifting my little finger, I would not." What if the Creator had chosen not to lift a finger; had not the will to bring forth this whole Creation, to love it, to preserve it, to continue to form and guide it toward wholeness and harmony?

We often think of the universe as a material construct, like a vast and highly intricate machine or a complicated puzzle, soulless and passion-less, governed by mathematics and physics, not alive but dead. We often think of the cosmos as a cold place in which, when something gets broken, it remains forever broken and disintegrates into nothingness with a cool Darwinian finality.

But, it is not always so. Nature heals. Many, if not most, diseases heal themselves over time with nothing more than simple resting and waiting. Study after study has verified this. Blood clots itself; broken bones do not remain broken, but knit themselves back together into a remarkable semblance of their proper form. With a little care wounds stop bleeding and disappear over time with nothing left but a scar. Any pruner knows if you cut a branch from a tree others grow back in its place. A huge forest scorched by a cataclysmic forest fire does not turn into a desert forever. It recovers naturally and comes back into health with new green pushing up through the charred coals.

Why do broken bones eventually knit up instead of remaining broken to cripple a creature once and for all? Why do wounds heal instead of bleeding forever? Why do forests regenerate after a fire or ice-storm instead of remaining barren until the end of time? Why does a great chaotic explosion at the birth of the universe come to order and harmony with planets and galaxies grandly circling to the music of the spheres through the ages?

We see compassion in other creatures, too.

In East Blue Hill a friend saw a flock of crows surround one of its number who had been hit by a car and push it gently out of the road. I've seen a flock of adult herring gulls come from nowhere and chase away a black-backed gull that was injuring one of their young [see below]. We have seen videos of whales and elephants taking care of their own injured or dying, or animals of one species adopting the young of another like the mother bear that adopted the beagle puppy a few years back.

Why? Because healing and compassion are embedded in the universe. In the beginning God willed that the Creation be made whole, and now that will to healing and wholeness is woven into the structure of the cosmos. The cosmos moves with a soul of compassion. The English essayist Alexander Pope, who was no stranger to astronomy and Newtonian physics, wrote in his *Essay on Man*, "The universe is one stupendous whole, whose body Nature is, and God the Soul."

I am not trying to get all mushy and sentimental here. I'm saying these things because I believe this is a question of life and death. If people see the universe as a compassionate and healing place they will be inclined to be compassionate and healing themselves and teach their children to be the same. If people see the universe as cruel and destructive they will act accordingly and teach their children to do the same.

One of the hardest questions I'm ever asked goes something like this: "How could God allow the Holocaust or Hiroshima, or the Vietnam War, or the killing fields of Cambodia, or the massacres in Rwanda, or 9/11, or war in Iraq, or the brutal repression in Syria, or the corona virus?" I hear this question over and over. I think there's an even deeper, unasked question here: "Who would want to love or be loved by a God who allows such horrors?"

Before we start blaming God for all the things that mankind does, let's stop and remember this. "The Lord said to Moses, 'I have set before you life and death; therefore choose life, that you and your people might live.'" We have the power to choose life or death, compassion or cruelty. God has not limited our capacity to do evil and to hurt any more than God has limited our capacity to do good and to heal. So when it comes to holocaust and genocide and war on civilians, we can't put this on God. We'd best not ask God to put a stop to these horrors unless we're ready to hear God ask us to do the same.

Just Folks

The Lord must love common-looking people;
He made so many of them

ATTRIBUTED TO ABRAHAM LINCOLN 1809-1865

WE ARE CHEERED by returning songbirds, even if they are of the most common varieties. When a dozen goldfinches mob the feeders and spangle the surrounding trees with yellow while waiting their turns, it is a delight to the heart, never mind that goldfinches are numerous everywhere. When crows drop in for popcorn we watch them with wonder for their sociability, for their cleverness, and simply for their pure and shimmering blackness, no matter that they are some of the most widespread birds on earth. When robins come a'worming we watch them with pleasure as they cock their heads, bob and bend, and draw a wiggling worm from the ground.

Even squabbling seagulls deserve a measure of respect for their stately elegance: their smart gray and white uniforms [impeccably clean despite all the garbage they eat], their brilliant yellow beaks with a bright red spot, their arrogant and withering gaze, their trumpeting call and their grand wingspread and gliding flight. If gulls were not so numerous, Audubon's apostles would come from all over just to observe them, but alas, there are just so many seagulls. Serious birders, it seems, must look for the more charismatic species, the endlessly confusing warblers, the rare thrushes and wrens and finches, the once-in-a-lifetime sightings. Still, the Lord must love common birds, too, because there are so many of them. Never mind the celebrity songbirds. We wouldn't trade one single bright and flittering goldfinch for six pallid Blackburnian warblers.

Shadbush [*Amelanchier spp*], also called juneberry, serviceberry and high-bush blueberry, comes into bloom about now with its delicate white star-shaped blossoms on a copper background. This shrub has served for thousands of years as a wilderness food. The First People dried the berries and pounded them together with venison to make pemmican that would keep unspoiled for months and provide protein and energy while on the trail. Also coming into bloom are various types of wild cherry including wild black cherry *Prunus serotina* and chokecherry *Prunus Virginiana*. Note that chokecherry can be poisonous to browsing animals.

These are all common things, but bearing an abundance of beauty and utility.

So, we find it odd how some admonish the poor and common people to simply work hard to get rich. These are often the same ones who were "born on third base and thought they hit a triple" or inherited wealth from their parents by accident of birth and will pass it on to their children. Calls to abolish inheritance taxes are coming from these same ones. The estate tax is as American as apple pie. It was instituted by our founders to prevent the growth of a wealthy aristocratic class, as in Europe, who would consolidate power and pass it on to their offspring regardless of how inept or lazy they might be. This was seen as Old World decadence. Nowadays, when it comes to real hard work, the common people beat the well-off hands down. Many must hold down two or three low-wage jobs just to make ends meet, while their work produces something of real value to others. So we need to hear no more admonishments from the wealthy that the common people should simply work harder, thank you very much.

FROM JOHN BOYLE O'REILLY 1844-1890:
It has always been the aim of royalty and aristocracy to lower the individual liberty and independence of the common people. A baron and a minuteman could not breathe the same air.

Angels Hovering 'Round

I WAS WALKING near the shore along the Friar Roads between Eastport and Campobello and saw a Great Black-backed gull brutally attacking a young gull less than half its size. The Black-backed was pecking viciously at the head of the younger gull and climbing up on its back trying to drown it. The buff wings of the smaller gull rose sodden and dripping from the water as the larger gull held it under. It seemed that the smaller gull was losing the struggle as it moved more and more slowly.

And then suddenly it all changed. Looking up I saw five full-grown gulls circling and calling above the horror in progress. Soon there were ten, then twenty, turning and circling overhead, witnessing and calling out the brutality of it. They did not dive or threaten or attack the attacker. But as the feathered host circled lower, the attacker abruptly lost its boldness and turned away from its victim, bobbing off innocently into the waves. To my great relief, the battered young gull composed itself, shook its head, and swam toward shore as other gulls dropped down and alighted gently and calmly in the water around it.

This is a true story, but, as Rebecca said to me, it is also a parable. Yes, there will always be suffering and the stronger will attack the weak. But, always and forever there will be witnesses shouting and calling out, moved with all the compassion, pity, anger and indignation of the cosmos. Though it may not *over*come every time, compassion will always *come*, hovering around again and again on healing wings.

From Split Rock to Standing Rock

TO THE SOUND of drumming and singing in Passamaquoddy, a crowd of close to 200 men, women and children gathered at Split Rock in Sipayik to support the Standing Rock Sioux peacefully resisting the construction of an oil pipeline way out West. Elders, adults, youth and children, Indian and non-Indian gathered around a bonfire by the bay sharing hot chocolate and cookies, smelling the wood smoke and cedar smudge. A circle dance began. A school bus unloaded chattering children from the reservation school holding signs that said "Water is Life" and "Split Rock to Standing Rock" while little ones chased each other laughing and gulls soared overhead. The drumming stopped and tobacco was passed around. A long prayer was offered in the tongue that has been spoken in that place for many thousands of years. It seemed as though the water was listening, and the rocks, and the islands, and the sky. Then several leaders spoke about the need to protect water and land. One speaker said, "We are different, we will not accept their values. Life is more than money. Water is more important than oil." Finally everyone walked quietly down over the multi-colored cobble beach to offer tobacco to the water.

The pipeline company says they own the land where the pipeline will go. They say that what they are doing is lawful; and they condemn the lawlessness of the protestors in resisting. But there is a higher law. When the Sioux Nation moved freely on the land, the water was pristine, the air was pure and the land was productive, providing for the needs of all the inhabitants. The land does not belong to the pipeline company. It does not belong to the Army Corps of Engineers. It does not belong to the tribe, either, for that matter. The land belongs to itself and to the Creator, and the soil and air and water must be protected for the well-being of all creatures. This is what it has come down to in our country today, tomorrow, and the day after. It is up to us. This is the struggle that will go on. This is why crowds of people from coast to coast and around the world are in the streets saying, "We do not accept their values; life is more than money; water is more important than oil."

FROM CHIEF JOSEPH 1840-1904:
Perhaps you think the Creator sent you here to dispose of us as you see fit… Do not misunderstand me, but understand me fully with reference to my affection for the land. I never said the land was mine to do with as I chose. The one who has the right to dispose of it is the one who has created it.

Lupine Revolution

THE SARDINE—a generic name for several types of herring—is the icon of Eastport, which calls itself 'the easternmost city in the USA.' It encompasses five islands, the largest being Moose Island. With a population of only about 1300 people, Eastport still remembers its heritage every New Year's Eve by dropping, not a sparkling ball, but a giant papier-mache sardine from the roof of the tallest building on Water Street. At its peak, Eastport had 5,000 people and dozens of sardine canneries in operation when the herring were running, and Eastport sardines were shipped around the world.

We first came to Eastport in the mid 70s while we were camping out on Cobscook Bay. We built a cabin on Leighton Neck in 1980. When I was called to serve the Congregational Church in Blue Hill in 1986, one of the many enticements, along with fields of lupine, was that our camp was only a little over two hours away. In the fall of 2014 we moved to Eastport year round just in time for Moose Island to get the coldest and snowiest winter ever recorded anywhere in the entire state of Maine.

The golden age for Eastport started to dim in the 1950s as the herring dwindled, the canneries began to close down and the city slipped into a depression, both economically and emotionally. There were few bleaker places along the Maine coast, and in the 70s Maine comedian Tim Sample joked about Eastport's Vacant Building Festival and quipped that if you could buy a Greyhound bus ticket with food stamps there would be no one left in Eastport. He could have said the same about most of Washington County.

Washington County's population in 2010 was 32,856; and declining. At 3,255 square miles, of which 695 square miles are water, the County is a good deal larger than Delaware. Due to the Native American population and a surprising number of Hispanic settlers who came to rake blueberries and stayed, the minority population is almost 10% compared to about 6% for the rest of Maine and fewer than 4% for neighboring Hancock County. There are many conservation lands notably Moosehorn National Wildlife Refuge at over 28,000 acres, Cobscook Bay State Park at 888 acres, and West Quoddy Head State Park at 541 acres, where you can hear the grumbling of softball-sized rocks being rolled up and down the beach by wind and waves coming up the Grand Manan Channel.

Economically, as of 2017 about 20% of the people in the Sunrise county were living below the federal poverty line compared to about 14% in Maine as a whole. According to Good Shepherd Food Bank, Washington County has a food insecurity rate of 17.6% and 28% of county children regularly face hunger. Unemployment in 2013 was 7.7% compared to 5.1% for the state. The suicide rate is 16.7 per 100,000, the third highest in the state.

Not long ago, I pulled into a gas station mini-mart way downeast on Route 1 for a cup of coffee and a blueberry muffin. I parked next to an older, banged-up Dodge Ram pick-up covered with a coating of oil and dust. In the bed were rubber boots, a chain-saw, some plastic fish totes, and numerous rusting tools—nothing unusual here where the pick-up trucks still outnumber the Subarus by about two to one.

What caught my eye was the vinyl lettering on the back window which read "In Loving Memory of Lillian _____ 1975-2015" with a photo beneath showing a haggard woman who could easily have been 65. With a bit of a shock I said to myself, "I know her." She used to call on the church for help with food and fuel, but as often as she called for herself, she called for someone else—her disabled brother, her mother- and father-in-law, her grown kids, her friends. I knew she had struggled through rehab into recovery and through chemotherapy into remission, but I didn't know that her struggles had ended so soon. As desperate as her situation was, she always looked out for her family and friends with a fierce determination and persistence. She was a grievous angel of hardship in far downeast Maine.

People stay on in Washington County for many reasons. Certainly, some stay because they lack the ambition or the resources even to move out. Many more stay because of family ties, ancestral history, a wide freedom to live your life, good fishing and hunting, and for just the sheer, raw beauty of it. It is very hard to describe this land of high tides and leaping whales, of shattered rocks and ripping currents, of eagles and herons, of sunrises and sunsets, to someone who hasn't seen it. It becomes a part of you, and you become a part of it. Elsewhere, humankind has the upper hand; here Nature still has the upper hand.

A living embodiment of that was Junior who made his living on the clam flats year round. The first time I met him he was coming up from the shore near our camp in his clean, but old, Toyota Tercel with some cement blocks in the back to give it traction, and several hods of squeaking clams. "I've been to the city, but I came right back. I wouldn't trade this for anything," he said with a sweeping gesture of his arm towards the bay. "I'm my own boss and I can pretty much do what I want to do." What he wanted to do was earn enough to make a living and send his children to college, and to be outside winter, spring, summer and fall. And that is just what he did.

That same self-sufficiency and independence shows itself when neighbor helps neighbor. It may be the coffee can on the check-out counter to help someone with medical bills, or the benefit supper to help the family whose house burned down, or the food pantries, the yard sales, the flea markets, or the deer meat that is brought to someone who can't hunt anymore. Compassion and hope are not dead. If anything, they burn brighter through hardship.

Comedians may joke, but it is no joke when years of poverty

from a collapsed economy bring high rates of domestic violence, suicide and petty crime along with despair and hopelessness and self-medication with alcohol and drugs to ease the pain. Drug use in Washington County has moved with terrifying speed from abuse of prescription opiates to the real thing: heroin. Most of us know the story. State funds for addiction treatment are drying up and law enforcement is stretched to the limit, particularly here where a small population is spread over a vast region, much of it in un-incorporated areas and tiny towns without any police force. The County Sheriff has only eight deputies patrolling an area half the size of Massachusetts.

I have a theory that Washington County may be a harbinger of all of post-apocalyptic America. It has been over-logged, over-fished, over-worked and overlooked. The former bounty of its rivers and forests and sea have been taken and hauled away to somewhere else; it has been exploited and left drained and depleted like a lot of other places in our great country. But it will not roll over and die.

Something new and startling has been happening here in the beleaguered easternmost county in Maine. After a number of false starts and dashed hopes over the years, Eastport is now over a dozen years into a remarkable rebirth which may provide a model for other forlorn and forgotten places. At its lowest, Eastport still had some resources, cheap real estate, a slower pace, soothing quiet, breath-taking beauty, and a good number of talented and devoted citizens, to mention a few. As all the other available coastal property was being bought up from Kittery to downeast, this area still had affordable old homes and saltwater farms, and people from elsewhere took notice.

Old houses have been renovated, vacant buildings have been filled, and Eastport is busier than it has been in 50 or 60 years. On any good day the sounds of hammers and saws echo around the island and trucks from the lumber yards rumble up and down the streets delivering materials.

The exodus of local young people from this region has not stopped, but it is increasingly being matched by the influx of older people from away—lupine lovers. Many of these people have fled other parts of Maine and the country to find a slower and more human pace of life. Many also bring talent and experience that can enrich the life of a community. Quaint and quirky shops open, galleries spring up, music and drama find a stage on which to appear. On the back roads, farmers and market gardeners take hold producing local food. People come from other places to be renewed. Where before there was despair and depression, now there are glimmers of hope. Maybe the apocalypse was not the end of the world. Maybe what we are seeing in Washington County is a rejection of the morbid Mad Max vision of post-apocalyptic America that is instead a slow, gradual healing.

In Machias there is the Beehive Collective using art for community building. In Whiting it's the indomitable Whiting Community School. In Trescott it is the Cobscook Institute offering broader educational opportunities for all ages. In Lubec it's the Sardine Museum, smokehouse and several new shops. In Edmunds you'll find Tide Mill Farm for organic meat, dairy and vegetables. In Pembroke the remarkable Pembroke Public Library offers books, talks and music. At Sipayik it is the monumental Passamaquoddy/Maliseet Dictionary and a school dedicated to passing on the native language. In Eastport you'll find the stalwart Quoddy Tides newspaper, the Commons, Peavey Library, the Eastport Arts Center, the Tides Institute and the Eastport Gallery boosting the creative culture of the area. These are just a few small parts of the spreading revival of Eastern Washington County.

You could call this the Lupine Revolution, and it is happening all over Maine, but most dramatically in some of its hardest-hit towns. It is significant that the lupine is the totemic flower of

Maine, especially since it is classified as an 'invasive species'. Lupine is attracted to what botanists call "disturbed soils." As an example, the lower fields on Blue Hill Mountain had been burned and sprayed with herbicides for commercial blueberry operations for many years until the mid-1990s. All that grew there were blueberries; the herbicides had killed everything else. The fields were eroded, rutted and the soil was depleted. When the land was put under conservation, the spraying stopped and pretty soon the lupine took hold. For several years they blanketed those worn-out fields with purple. People flocked to see the lupine, they took pictures, had picnics, weddings and festivals.

Lupine is a legume which puts down a tough and deep root system with the ability to fix nitrogen in the soil where it grows. A stand of lupine moving into a field of worn-out soil will soon improve it so that other plants can move in too, native and non-native. After a few years, something strange happens; the lupine begins to shrink back to a few smaller patches while the native flora fill in and take over. After a time a healthy diverse flora and fauna are once more established and flourishing.

This is what the Lupine Revolution is doing in so many of our small coastal towns: rebuilding the soil, and the soul, of forgotten Maine.

Trying to Be Good

One misty, moisty morning when cloudy was the weather;
I chanced to see an old man clothed all in leather,
Clothed all in leather with his hat under his chin,
How do you do, and how do you do, and how do you do again?

NURSERY RHYME

WE'RE IN THAT SWEET ZONE now between the first flowers blooming and the first biting insects emerging. When the drizzle lets up we can work in the garden or the field in relative comfort—still cool during the day and just chilly enough during the night. But come Mother's Day or thereabouts we can expect the return of mosquitoes and black flies on warmer, calmer days, just the sort of weather that the bees need to do their work of pollinating the apples and blueberries. A great deal depends on some warm sunny weather during the bloom. If it is too misty, moisty and cloudy, the bees will stay home from work, and the harvest will be the poorer for it, like last year when we had a dreary May and hardly an apple to be seen around here come September.

According to reports, researchers are comparing modern weather data to Thoreau's journals and estimating that Spring is coming to the Northeast about 11 days earlier than it did in 1850. You'll hear no complaints from me about that. The optimistic among us have turned over their gardens and planted peas already. The more skeptical wonder what good it does to plant now when we may have several more weeks of drear.

Still, Spring is rolling in as it always does; that's something we can always count on. In other ways the world is more uncertain, what with climate change, pandemics, explosions in Texas, floods along the Mississippi, earthquakes in China, catastrophes in Bangladesh and whatever the next disaster *de jour* will be. It seems that they follow after each other like the waves on Schoodic Point until we might wonder where the whole world is headed.

But let's take the long view for a moment. Look at the world "from a distance" the way the Creator might see it. Wars have not ceased, but after millennia of war as a way of life, fatalities in war have fallen drastically and there has not been a major conflict between multiple nations in over 75 years. This is unprecedented. Though not entirely eliminated, slavery is no longer legal anywhere. Though women still suffer abuse in some places, their right to vote is established in more and more countries. Civil rights regardless of race, gender, age, economic status or sexual orientation are becoming the world-wide standard. This was unthinkable even a hundred years ago.

There is a power at work in the Creation that wants justice, righteousness and peace. How do I know? History tells me so. As Theodore Parker, Dr King and others have said, "The moral arc of the universe is long, but it bends toward justice." History is proving them right. Maine writer and philosopher Zoe Weil wrote shortly after the Boston Marathon bombings, "Let's remember this: For every person who is evil, there are countless people who are deeply kind. For every murderer, there are people coming to the aid of strangers in droves. For every act of senseless violence, there are thousands of acts of meaningful goodness."

Or as Maine author Sandy Phippen said it, "People are just trying to be good." And Sandy was mostly right, you know.

Memorial Day

When lilacs last in the dooryard bloom'd.
And the great star early droop'd in the western sky at night,
I mourn'd, and yet shall mourn with ever-returning spring...

FROM WALT WHITMAN

REMEMBERING AND GRIEVING the dead is natural and good for us, and many other creatures do the same. That is what we Americans do on Memorial Day weekend. On Sunday we go to the cemeteries where departed friends and family rest quietly under stones while new, translucent leaves flag the branches of the oaks and maples overhead, pink and white phlox runs riot through the grass underfoot, and bluets and violets silently set their faces toward the sun for their brief moment of glory.

A walk in the woods reveals to the wondering eye clusters of rare and delicate Trillium in bloom. Nearby, spears of blue flag rise from the mud, and Rhodora, New England's wild azalea, is covered in shocking pink bloom. Ox-eye daisies are raising their gold and white early blooms above scalloped deep green leaves while magenta Lady-slippers and blue and white Forget-me-nots show their shy flowers in shady places. Apples, pears, and lilacs are in bloom while wild cherries and shadbush petals are falling. Life into death into life.

It's a very good thing that we do; though it probably does us more good than it does those who have gone on beyond this world of joy and pain. Then, on Monday we honor those who have died in war. That is good too. After all, they were promised that their ultimate sacrifice was pure and right and for the benefit of the living, and that we would ever honor it. Even if they were deceived by leaders who were not sent into harm's way themselves, nor their sons, are we to forget that promise after the dead are gone? A few veterans have hung flags on the utility poles in some towns, and that is good too: but not an unblemished good. The flags are made in China. They get soaked in rain and splashed with mud by big trucks, and they hang sodden and unappreciated in the night. Far more veterans stay home and grieve for their buddies and themselves, for the endless devastations of war inflicted on warriors and innocents alike, and for the hollow and deceitful promises of peace through slaughter.

And what might the dead say on Memorial Day from their vantage point in a realm far away from our ancient hostilities of races, religions and nations, but still so near to our hearts? "Did you honor us like this when we were alive? Did you take our children by the hand and see that they had enough? Did you love us then as much as you do now? Why do you not offer your flags and flowers and food and prayers for the living? We are gone on, safe in the hands of the Creator, but the living are yet in your hands. Spend your billions and trillions on food not on firebombs, on schools not on shells, on medicine not on missiles. Make the ultimate sacrifice so that others may live, not so that they may die at your hands. That is the sort of honor we dead desire for ourselves: But even more... for you."

FROM DWIGHT D. EISENHOWER:
Every gun that is made, every warship launched, every rocket fired signifies in the final sense a theft from those who hungry and are not fed, those who are cold and not clothed.

AND FROM HELEN KELLER:
Although the world is full of suffering, it is also full of the overcoming of it.

Wasting Our Inheritance

IN LUKE'S STORY of the prodigal son a young man asks for his inheritance from his father so that he can go out into the world and seek his fortune, but what he really does is go out in the world to party, and he quickly spends all of his birthright. That means there is no more where that came from. The young man ends up penniless, caring for someone else's pigs which, for a Jew, would be a miserable job since pigs are considered unclean.

One day he realizes that his father's servants are living better than he is with bread enough and to spare. So he returns home, admitting his wrong and asking to live as one of his father's servants. The father welcomes his son home and puts on a feast for him, whereupon the steadfast and thrifty older brother is upset. The father calms him by reassuring him that he will get everything as his inheritance. And so the story ends.

Like all parables, the story of the Prodigal Son is not just about a son asking forgiveness from his father and his father giving it, though it is about that. This story could also be about us and God: God gives out of love and we take out of selfishness and greed and blow it. But God is always willing to forgive if we are willing to change our ways and ask forgiveness.

The story of the prodigal son could also be about us and the earth, and I want to look at that a little more closely. When this story was first told, no one was talking about exploitation and depletion of natural resources, mass extinctions of species, the population carrying capacity of the planet or parts-per-million of carbon dioxide in the atmosphere. But a good parable can be about much more than itself. A good parable has a fractal quality allowing it to change scale through space and time without losing its truth and to be about the smallest things at the same time as being about the largest things. That is what this parable does.

If this parable is about us and the earth [what previous generations would have called God's Providence and Creation], then we are the wandering young prodigal and the Creator is the father, and our squandered inheritance is the bounty of the earth.

This recalls Job who says it this way: "...Is it by your wisdom that the hawk soars, and spreads his wings to the south? Is it at your command that the eagle mounts up and makes his nest on high?"

For most of the history of humankind, long before the major world religions appeared, the earth and its bounty were seen as coming to us as a birthright from our Creator, a gift of God's grace, to be husbanded with care and to be passed on undiminished to the next generation. If the gift was honored, there would be bread enough and to spare, not only for us, but for those generations who would come after us.

Yet what does the prodigal son do with his inheritance? The King James Bible says, "[T]he younger son gathered all together and took his journey into a far country and there wasted his substance with riotous living." As an aside, one might wish that Luke the great storyteller had gone into a little more detail here about this riotous living business. Luke did not, but generations of painters and preachers have filled in the details from their vivid and sometimes lascivious imaginations. One thinks of Rembrandt's 1637 *The Prodigal Son in a Tavern* wherein a young man in 17th century dress, who looks very much like the artist himself, holds a young woman on his lap and raises a tankard in his right hand. You get the picture.

And what have we prodigals done with the Creation we received as our inheritance the instant we were born and that cost us nothing? We have wasted its substance with riotous living. Without going into the juicy details let's just say that industrial nations now have the highest standard of living in human history while at the same time the planet is in a sorely diminished condition; the fisheries are rapidly depleting, the forests are being decimated, the air is befouled and the water is polluted more than ever before. Can we continue to live this way? Clearly not; we have wasted the substance of our inheritance on riotous living.

The turning point for the prodigal son came when he realized that he was living far worse than his father's hired servants, and resolved to go back, ask forgiveness, and offer to serve his father as they did. This change of heart is the climax of the story. Without this *metanoia*, this 'born again' experience of the prodigal, none of the rest could have happened. The homecoming, the forgiveness, the welcoming feast all depend on the young man's change of heart.

One of the most powerful renderings of the return of the prodigal is Rembrandt's poignant painting from around 1667 where the prodigal, dressed in dirty tattered rags and sole-less shoes, has fallen on his knees in front of his richly dressed father while the father leans over with his hands on the young man's shoulders to comfort him. The yawning, aching gulf of separation between father and son has been crossed, the wounds between them are being healed and the bonds are being renewed.

We feel that ache when we see the results of our wasting of the Creation: the ravaging of resources, the extinction of species, the melting ice, the soaring carbon dioxide. We feel the loneliness of our riotous lifestyles and the desperation of what will surely happen if we do not change our hearts.

Can the earth forgive us and welcome us home again as the father did his prodigal son? It is my conviction that the change of heart is underway, that we are beginning to close the gulf of separation between us and this marvelous Creation that was prepared to receive us the instant we were born, that we are beginning to heal the wounds that we have inflicted, and renew the bonds that were broken.

The age-old parable of the prodigal son shows clearly how this can be done: by our own change of heart, by turning away from wasting our substance in riotous living and trying to be Masters of the Universe, and by turning toward being servants of the Creator and the Creation. Only then will there be bread enough and to spare, not just for a few of us, but for all of us. One by one, by the hundreds, by the thousands, by the millions, there is still time for us to come home to this fair Creation always prepared to receive us.

Being Bees

In smiling days and sunny hours, the busy Bee from vernal flowers
Sips nectar sweet and well supplies/his feet with pollen, a fragrant prize...
Hence learn, my youthful friends, to weigh/and fix the worth of every day;
In life's fair prime your stores increase, that hoary age may pass in peace.

JONATHAN FISHER, 1834

BLOOMS OF ASH, MAPLE AND OAK have gone by but the pines are still in flower. Their tassels emerge from buds on last year's growth and are 3-4" inches long and covered with pollen. In some areas this yellow dust coats the surface of ponds and puddles, not to mention your car's windshield. If you are having coughing and sneezing fits these days, you can likely blame Maine's state flower, the white pine cone and tassel. In the fields while dandelions and bluets go to seed, buttercups and daisies are coming into bloom. Along roadways and on poor and disturbed soil the unofficial Maine floral emblem, the lovely lupine, is coming into bloom with its tall spires turning purple, pink, blue and even white. If you are especially lucky on an early June day, you may even see a tiger swallowtail butterfly flutter by.

If insects can feel happiness, it is safe to guess that there are several million happy bees darting and dancing from flower to flower through the fields and orchards and blueberry barrens these days. Watching a honeybee or bumble bee nuzzle up to a fertile blossom and do its ecstatic dance among the petals is sure evidence that they are seriously partying down. In a dance that has been performed for eons, the flower beguiles the bee with its intoxicating perfume and the bee rewards the flower by gathering its pollen and spreading it far and wide. What reason is there to think that this does not feel exquisitely pleasurable to both? Some 60,000 hives of honeybees *Apis mellifera* are trucked in to Maine to pollinate fruits and berries in the Spring. Truckloads and truckloads of joy.

One orchard I worked in ages ago got its hives each Spring from an old man named Louie. He said his last name rhymed with "unconscious" so we just called him Louie Unconscious. The dilapidated beehives were held together with tin, tarpaper and wire, and so was the old truck he brought them in on. Every now and then one of the hives would disintegrate as we lifted it off the truck and we would run like the blue blazes through the blooming apple trees with clouds of angry bees behind.

Unfortunately, honey bees today are endangered by *colony collapse disorder* that has devastated domestic hives. Evidence points *to neonicotinoid* pesticides, whose use increases yearly, as the root of the problem. In self-defense, pesticide manufacturers blame the *varroa* mite which attacks bees in the hive. More likely, the pesticides weaken the hive and the mites finish the job. The European Union has taken the matter seriously enough to pass legislation limiting the use of these pesticides.

Maine also has at least 270 species of wild bees that help with pollination, according to the University of Maine. At least 40 of these species work the blueberries. Did you know this? There are 15 native Maine species of the well-known bumblebee *Apis bomba*. One of these is even managed commercially for blueberry pollination. Bumblebees are particularly well suited for the Maine climate as they can raise their body temperature above that of their surroundings enabling them to reproduce in colder conditions than other bees. Just like any Mainer, really.

FROM EDWARD ABBEY:
This flower is irresistibly attractive… I have yet to look into one and not find a honeybee or bumblebee wallowing drunkenly inside, powdered with pollen, glutting itself on what must be a marvelous nectar. You can't get them out of there—they won't go home… Until closing time.

Keep Them Alive Upon the Earth

THE STORY OF THE FLOOD is one of the best-known of our entire Western tradition, and it appears in many other traditions worldwide. It has been the subject of story, song, and art wherever it is told. In the beginning God created humans and animals and declared them good. But things started to go bad. The creatures, particularly humans, were wicked and "every inclination of the thoughts of their hearts was only evil continually." So God decided to "blot out from the earth" with a great flood all the creatures save the Noah family selected by God and pairs of every kind of creature selected by the Noah family.

God tells Noah to save pairs of every creature to "keep their kind alive upon the earth." God's desire to save every species is central to the story. After the flood, God makes a covenant with Noah to never again "destroy every living creature." "As long as the earth endures, seedtime and harvest, cold and heat, summer and winter, day and night shall not cease." This covenant is sealed with a rainbow in the sky. A beautiful story, a version of one of the most widely told myths on earth.

> *Then God said to Noah and his children, "I am establishing a covenant with you and your descendants after you and with every living creature, the birds and every animal of the earth... that never again shall all flesh be cut off..."*

What to say about it? I'm going to suggest that there are at least four underlying truths about the nature of the universe embodied in this myth. But to understand we must go more than skin deep. We've had enough of skin-deep theology, we need some theology with some flesh to it, some meat to it.

The first truth embedded here is that *there is a continuing right and good order to the universe*—seedtime and harvest, summer and winter, day and night; that the Creation is not entirely chaotic or random, but that it follows certain orderly and predictable ways.

Second, *humans have an effect on the rest of Creation*; that our actions can bring harm or benefit to the entire Creation.

Third, *the Creator desires to keep every kind of creature alive upon the earth.*

And last, *the Creator will enter into covenant with us and the future if we will act faithfully* toward the Creation. These are the truths of this story.

Here we come to a crisis. The story of Noah's ark is so fantastic, so Disneyesque, so long overdone in children's books, B movies, inferior Sunday School lessons, cartoons, skits, jokes, and more, that we are very likely to tuck it away in a mental file labeled *Children's Myths, Superstitions and Fables: Do Not Take Seriously.*

"Two of every species on earth on a boat 350 feet long built with primitive hand tools by three men in a few days? Come on. A god who brings order to the cosmos, and wants every kind of creature to stay alive upon the earth? No way. Humans whose actions and attitudes affect the whole biosphere? Get serious." In our rationality, we reject it all, and out goes the baby with the bathwater.

If we reject the whole story, then we risk rejecting the four underlying truths about the nature of the universe. First, we reject the notion that the universe has a natural order that will move in certain ways, mysterious or predictable. Second, we reject the idea that humans can have any real effect, good or bad, on this natural order. Third, we reject the idea of a Creator who cares what happens to the living things on earth. And fourth, we reject the notion of a God who will enter into covenant with us for generations to come.

Once we do that, we're left with these conclusions: that we live in the midst of disorder, random destruction and chaos; that our actions are essentially meaningless so we may as well do whatever gives us quick pleasure; that it does not matter if we wipe the animals out or wipe ourselves out; that there is no God who created and cares about us and the animals or nothing really sacred in the universe; and that there is nothing we can do for our children, grandchildren and future generations. Now isn't that pretty much what we fear in the culture around us, a rising flood of meaninglessness, alienation, chaos, and violence?

That is precisely why we return to this story again and again. We aren't returning to the impossible belief that Noah and his sons built a ship that was big enough to hold specimens of every species of animal to ride out the tempestuous waters of a great flood covering the whole earth. We are returning to the truth of the faithfulness of God through age after age, covenant after covenant, from that day to this. We are returning to the truth of a God declaring that all living things are precious, and declaring that our small acts do affect the whole earth, a God always willing to forgive and preserve future generations to keep them alive upon the earth.

This may be as close as we can come to answering the question we started with: Does the Bible elevate man above the earth, or the earth above man? From what we have seen, the answer is clearly "Neither one nor the other." The upshot here is that God is concerned with preserving the earth, yes, and humankind, yes, and every other creature equally as well, that is why God put us all in the same boat, so to speak. That is the conclusion we are led to draw from the ancient and honored Flood stories.

Is there anything we would not dare to do to keep future generations alive upon the earth? "If we do not now dare everything," wrote James Baldwin years ago, "the fulfillment of that prophecy, re-created from the Bible in song by a slave, is upon us: *God gave Noah the rainbow sign, No more water, the fire next time!*"

We Will Live

IF YOU ARE STILL WITH ME, then we have rambled together through a whole year, at least on paper, and through the countryside along the coast of Maine and beyond, sometimes wandering off the path, sometimes stopping to observe and chat, always looking around— above, below, behind, before, beside and within. This sort of ramble is what we humans have been doing ever since we first got up on our hind legs a million years ago—walking and talking outside under the sky. It's healthy, and it stimulates the heart and the imagination.

This is a good thing, because imagination is an essential survival skill for looking beyond the next turn in an unknown trail. Drawing on our experience and others', on the visions of our prophets, on the traditions of our ancestors, and on our own imaginations, we envision how we may walk the rest of the way ahead. No one can see the future, but we can imagine our way there.

In 587 B.C. the Jewish people were scattered into exile, their religion disintegrated, and their institutions destroyed. Death was all around them. Ezekiel the prophet had a vision. And the Spirit said to Ezekiel, "Man, can these bones live?" And Ezekiel answered, "O God, You know." The Spirit said, "Prophesy to the wind, man, and say to the breath, 'Come from the four winds, O Spirit, and breathe upon these dead that they may live.' Prophesy and say to the bones, 'God says, I will raise you from your graves of death, my people, and bring you home.' So Ezekiel prophesied." In two short generations, the people returned home and there began an unprecedented flowering of their faith and culture. From the stark and chilling visions of Ezekiel grew the beautiful and unparalleled poetry of Isaiah, and from Isaiah grew the preaching of Jesus that transformed the West, and is still doing so.

After the fall of Rome, Dark Ages followed, an epoch characterized by the forgetting of classical ideals of democracy and humanity, constant warfare, widespread illiteracy even among royalty, and virtual slavery for the masses. Then, rather suddenly in the 14th century a rebirth of art, music, religion, and science and the rediscovery of classical ideals swept across Europe. It was called the spirit of the "Renaissance" but it could just as well have been called the spirit of the "Resurrection."

In 1890 when Native American tribes had been deprived of life and liberty and land, when native children were torn from their families and punished for speaking their own language or following their own faith, when native culture was stolen and placed in museums and universities, a great spiritual revival swept the western tribes. Through the Ghost Dance exiled and conquered people began to dream dreams and see visions and prophesy. They sang, "Yani'tsini'hawana" "We shall live again!" The resulting Pan-Indian movement brought together indigenous people from coast to coast and now all over the world the songs and wisdom of native faith are changing the hearts of even their former oppressors. The spirit of our Mother the Earth—so long neglected in favor of our Father in the Sky—is being resurrected in the hearts and minds of millions.

When we see our institutions falling around us we know that for all of our nation's power and wealth and advanced technology, we too may be a people in exile, our traditions under siege, our faith threatened. It is not too soon for us to undertake our own visions and dreams. It is not too soon to prophesy to our own people like Ezekiel and Isaiah and Jesus and the prophets of the Ghost Dance: "God says, 'I will raise you from the dead and bring you home.'" "We will live, we will live."

But if we live to see this resurrection, we know well that it will not be by the might of the sword or the power of money, nor by human technology or intelligence alone. It will not be by cell phones and space satellites, nor by international treaties and trade agreements. It will not be by the spirit of some supernatural, omnipotent, omniscient kingly God above. If we live to see a resurrected world, it will be by the very same Spirit that raised the dry bones. It will be by the Spirit in each of us, the spirit of love for each other, and for our whole blue-green earth.

FROM GHOST DANCE SONGS COLLECTED BY
ETHNOLOGIST JAMES MOONEY C. 1890:

The earth—the crow, the earth—the crow
The crow brought it with him, the crow brought it with him.

My father, I am poor; my father, I am poor
Our father is about to take pity on me,
Our father is about to make me fly around

My children, my children
Here it is, I hand it to you
The earth, the earth.

Acknowledgements

IT WOULD BE IMPOSSIBLE to thank everyone who helped bring this book into being, but I want to mention David Snyder and Kathy Melio at WERU-FM who first saw the Almanack's fitness for radio, Nat Barrows at Penobscot Bay Press and Edward French at the Quoddy Tides who saw its appeal for regional newspapers, John Hanson of *Maine Boats, Homes & Harbors* magazine who took it to a national level, and Bill Henderson of *Pushcart Press* who published it in book form. Gratitude to you all.

To the faithful of the Blue Hill Congregational Church, for the triumphs and failures, for the laughter and tears through the years, I thank you. Most of all, I thank my wife, first reader, recording engineer, and huge fan from the beginning, Rebecca Haley McCall. Some of my best one-liners are stolen from her.

One of the many joys of this work is hearing from readers and listeners who are filled with that love and delight in their own corner of Creation. They extend far beyond Maine through New England, the South, the Midwest and Plains, the West Coast, Canada and as far away as the UK and New Zealand. From all these places come back observations of the natural world, sensations of light, colors, scents and sounds, descriptions of lively creatures, and feelings of wonder and adoration for the beauty of it all.

I hear about how people pull their cars over on the way to work on Friday mornings to listen to the Almanack on the radio, how they stream it live when traveling in far lands, how families gather old and young around on Sunday mornings to catch the latest, as though going to church, and how the family dog howls along with the radio at the end. I hear how *Small Misty Mountain* and *Great Speckled Bird* rest on people's night-stands to be the last thing read at night or the first thing in the morning.

All of you are co-authors with me.

My gratitude to every one.

Bibliographical Notes

INTRODUCTION

Holy Bible, King James Version, 1611. We have occasionally taken liberties with the translation for the sake of clarity.

Tao Teh Ching, by Lao-Tzu, translated by John Wu, Shambhala, 1990

Tao Te Ching, by Lao Tzu, translated by Gia-fu Feng & Jane English, 1989

Old Farmer's Almanac, Yankee Inc., Dublin, New Hampshire 2020 edition

Farmer's Almanac, Geiger Bros., Lewiston, Maine 2020 edition

New Farmer's Almanac, Greenhorns, Ltd. W. Pembroke, Maine 2020 edition

Annie Dillard, *Teaching a Stone to Talk*, 1982, Holy the Firm, 1977

Walt Whitman, *Leaves of Grass*, 1855

Thomas Paine, *Age of Reason*, 1794

Henry David Thoreau, *Journals*, 1837-1861, *Walden*, 1854, *Faith in a Seed* 1993

SUMMER

Charles Darwin, *Voyage of the Beagle*, 1839, 1905, *Origin of Species*, 1859

George Washington Carver, source of quote unknown, found at *Goodreads*

William Butler Yeats, *The Town* 1928, *The Land of Heart's Desire*, 1894

Kung Fu-tzu or "Confucius", *Analects*, 3rd century BCE

Bella Abzug, source of quote unknown, found at *Goodreads*

Okute, *Touch the Earth*, T.C. McLuhan ed., 1988

John Muir, *A Thousand Mile Walk to the Gulf*, 1916

Brother Lawrence, *The Practice of the Presence of God*, 1692

Chicago Mass Choir, *"You Can't Hurry God"*

Thich Nhat Hanh, *Mindfulness Gathas*, 2008

Hasidic saying, *Earth Prayers*, Roberts and Amidon eds., 1991

Rachel Carson, *The Sense of Wonder*, 1965

Bernd Heinrich, *One Man's Owl*, 1994

AUTUMN

Wei Yingwu, *An Autumn Night Message to Qiu*, Witter Bynner, translator

Hsiao Kang, quote source unknown

Pope Francis, *Vatican Press Release*, June 7, 2013

Edwin Way Teale, *A Walk Through the Year*, Library of Nature Classics, 1978

Mary Oliver, *Song for Autumn*, 2005

Elizabeth Lawrence, source of quote unknown, found at *Goodreads*

Dorothy Livesay, source unknown, found at *Goodreads*

Max Planck, *Where Is Science Going?* 1932

Robert Frost, *The Star-splitter,* 1923

Sojourner Truth, *The Narrative of Sojourner Truth,* 1850

Richard Jeffries, *The Life of the Fields,* 1884

Ralph Waldo Emerson, *Nature: Addresses and Lectures,* 1841

Dorothy Lee, *Freedom and Culture,* Spectrum, 1961

Aldo Leopold, *A Sand County Almanac and Other Writings...,* 1941

George Eliot, *Letter to Miss Lewis,* 1841

Flavius Josephus, *The Jewish War,* c. 75 AD

WINTER

Gary Lawless, *Caribouddism,* Florian Schultz-Sierra Club, 1998

Carol Dana "Red Hawk Pipikwass," *While No One Was Looking,* Little
Letterpress, Knox, Maine 1989

Margaret Mead, no source found, probably public domain

Robert Quillen, *Literary Digest [?],* c. 1930

Henry Wadsworth Longfellow, *Christmas Bells,* in *Our Young Folks,* 1865

Gilbert Keith Chesterton, *What's Wrong with the World?* 1910

Margaret Fuller, source unknown, found at *Goodreads*

Ambrose Bierce, *Devil's Dictionary,* 1911

Hosea Ballou, *An Examination of the Doctrine of Future Retribution,* Boston, 1834

John Scotus Eriugena, *Periphyseon,* 9th century AD

Terry Tempest Williams, *Refuge,* 2001

William Penn, *Fruits of Solitude,* 1778

Anonymous, *The Cloud of Unknowing,* Late 14th century AD

Zoe Weil, *Most Good, Least Harm,* 2009

Donald Culross Peattie, source unknown, found at *Goodreads*

John Banister Tabb, *Phantoms,* 1906

Eudora Welty, source unknown, found at *Goodreads*

Dr Martin Luther King Jr, *I've Been to the Mountaintop,* April 3, 1968

SPRING

Henry Beston, *The Northern Farm: A Glorious Year on a Small Maine Farm* 1948

Luther Standing Bear, *Touch the Earth,* T.C. McLuhan ed., 1988

Julian of Norwich, *A Book of Showings to the Anchoress Julian...,* c. 1375

Richard Powers, *The Overstory,* W.W. Norton Company, NY 2018

Ellen DeGeneres, source refrigerator magnet

Anatole France, source unknown, found at *Goodreads*

William Shakespeare, *As You Like It*, 1599

Henry David Thoreau, *Journals* 1837-1861

E. O. Wilson, *Consilience*, 1998

Robert Frost, *Two Tramps in Mud Time*, 1934

David Mallett, Maine songwriter, *Greenin' Up Real Good*

Pope Francis, Encyclical letter, *Laudato si'*, May 24, 2015

St Francis of Assisi, *Canticle of the Sun*, 1224

Abraham Lincoln, [Lincoln's historical statements are well-documented, but his aphorisms are notoriously hard to pin down. He is incorrectly attributed more often than even Yogi Berra]

John Boyle O'Reilly, quoted in *Shillelagh* by John Hurley, 2007

Chief Joseph, *Touch the Earth*, T.C. McLuhan ed., 1988

Sandy Phippen, *People Trying to be Good*, 1991

Dwight D Eisenhower, *Cross of Iron*, speech in Washington DC, April 16, 1953

Helen Keller, *Optimism*, 1903

Jonathan Fisher, *Scripture Animals*, self-published 1834

Edward Abbey, *Desert Solitaire*, 1968

James Mooney, *The Ghost Dance Religion…* Smithsonian, 1899